MY BABIES, MY PROMISE

The Journey of My Soul

THE LOUISE SULLIVAN STORY

To those who selflessly care for, foster and adopt the unwanted children of this world.

CONTENTS

Foreword

In February 2020, I came into possession of a 580-page typewritten story written by Nanny, my great-grandmother, over 100 years ago and tucked away for many years, unknown to most in my family. With the Coronavirus pandemic just beginning, I suddenly found myself under a "stay at home" order, with lots of time to read this document. Upon completion, I immediately decided that this was a story that needed to be told.

Nanny was an amazing woman with a heart filled with love...love for 168 babies whom she fed, clothed, bathed and "mothered" over a 12-year period from 1915-1927. She never took one penny for any of her "baby work," but felt directed by God to care for her babies. Three doctors brought unwanted babies to Nanny for her loving care; then she found homes for her babies with wealthy families, initially in

Chicago, IL and subsequently in Pasadena, CA. Nanny devoted her work to God, felt guided by Him to do her "baby work," and dedicated her baby nursery to the memory of her biological son, Kenzie, who died at age 17 from diphtheria. In reading Nanny's story, I immediately felt a connection with my great-grandmother who passed away when I was just eight years old. Having a strong faith myself, I felt deeply connected to Nanny and to fulfilling her desire to share her story with the world.

Upon sharing this treasure with a cousin, we became committed to unfolding the story Nanny wanted to share but never did. Along the way, we connected with two of the adult children of the last two of Nanny's babies. The four of us became determined to make Nanny's dream come true. Along the way, three of Nanny's grandchildren, two of whom are in their 90's, gave insight into Nanny's life through their personal experiences with her. While simple editing was within our capabilities, organizing this story from her stream-of-consciousness format into a readable book became a daunting task. We are incredibly grateful to our outstanding editor who helped us tell Nanny's Story in a concise, cohesive manner. We are also extremely appreciative to our many family and friends for their generous donations in making this story become a reality.

This story is more than a treasure for our family legacy. We also hope this book will reach the families of Nanny's babies to help them understand how each child was a treasure to her and a blessing from God. Perhaps this book might lead to connecting those whom Nanny mothered and facilitating connections with even more family. This is a story all will want to read...a story of how one woman's faith and devotion can make a difference in the life of a child.

Nancy Brown

Enjoy this inspiring story,

your friend,

Nancy

Introduction

In no way are these pages to be treated or looked upon as a sensational novel. Had I not been directed by an inner voice that I call the voice of God, I would even hesitate to tell strangers of the future that I lived. Keeping that knowledge veiled and suddenly thrusting it upon the reader as a climax would not be treating my story with due reverence. I am not a scholar, nor even a reader. Hence, I am handicapped, at least in an author's sense. However, in building a memorial to my son, who passed from this plane in July 1915, I have learned many things that I once considered impossible.

If I had to equate my story to a fairy tale, perhaps "The Little Old Lady Who Lived in a Shoe" would be a good fit. However, that lighter vein could not continue throughout the story. The undercurrent that no one has ever known or consequently understood — not even my own children — has been so replete with heartache and sadness that I could hardly live. I could merely state facts. But with some training, I was able to manufacture a happy frame of mind. I was able to rise above my situation and glimpse the resultant good of every situation. I was able to see that this life is not a haphazard affair and that each individual, possessing the wonderful privilege of being born, plays a part to improve it.

There would be no story without the pain of losing my son, Kenzie. At times, it felt that my heart would break. But my intense sorrow was nothing in comparison to the bursting of newborn love that follows when acting as God directs. It makes one strong to learn how to look at life the right way. After all I endured — all the pain and heartache — I came out of the fracas as strong as a lion. Now, I cannot think of a combination of events that could scare me. And I speak from actual experience, which in my mind is the only knowledge worth having.

I have always wondered why God was so good to me. To make me different, to make me want to work when I did not have to, and to make me want to get in touch with human hearts when I could have taken a check and been relieved of further responsibility. Just *why*? Only God knows my sincere thankfulness for his constant encouragement.

There are many reasons for my clinging steadfastly to God. Long before I finished my baby work, it dawned on me that God is the only one capable of seeing into the heart of mankind. To me, this realization represented the only time in my adult life that I was given a "square deal." Little wonder that I stuck to the last ditch, willing to die knowing that I have not lived in vain. My service has been accepted as I have offered it: a work of love and sacrifice for the benefit of mankind.

Who knows whether I followed a recognized religion or one suited to my own way of thinking? All I know is that my faith has produced an inner satisfaction that I wish I could pass to every person who feels distress or gropes in the dark.

I have lived the latest chapter of my life in my own home — four being spent in Chicago and eight in California — where I have experienced a Communion between God and myself. My "babies" have been the tentative means of communication. While God kept me concentrated and well-supplied with His darling little representatives, He has aroused my spiritual senses. Hitherto, I made the discovery of an unknown possession: my Spiritual Radio. Unknowingly, I picked up the wave-length that enabled me to hear, and under certain conditions, to pierce the ether.

This life, in my interpretation, is an opportunity to improve oneself with the tools at one's command. Every deed is recorded, just as in our school days when we discover whether we sit at the head or the foot of the class. Do you see then, according to my deductions and beliefs, the necessity of making one's actions count for something worthwhile? Connecting this thought to my baby work, each life that I saved prepared me to meet my Maker, along with my father, mother, and child. The more faithful service that I gave, the stronger I became to meet the challenges of my post. When I took a baby, it was for the betterment of that baby — not for a selfish motive.

Not once in my life have I felt that I was breaking a law, though many accused me of doing so. My undercurrent has always been a sincere desire to serve God, and humanity has benefited from my actions. Whenever I had the misfortune of meeting a questioning welfare worker, I always felt it was an imposition and got through with it as politely and with as few words as possible. I had to accept that this world does not permit those with high ideals to exist without strenuous resistance — especially when those individuals are "ordinary women." What has always tickled me is the fact that after doing quite a bit of shouting, the public very considerately let me resume my work and carry my responsibilities.

This being a material age, it becomes rather difficult to advance spiritually. Luckily, I have inherited the ability to stay on one track indefinitely. Loyalty and faithfulness were outstanding features of both of my parents, and such traits have aided in my life's work.

I have learned — somewhat indirectly — that my evident willingness to perform my baby work has been a source of befuddlement. In fact, I cannot count the number of people who cannot understand what I do.

"Why does she do this menial work?" someone recently

asked a neighbor of mine. "What's it all about? How can she keep at it continually?"

All of these detractors share a sanctimonious air towards one who could stoop to anything so lowly.

"Just think of it," they seem to say. "She puts those slum babies in her own bath and washes them herself. Those filthy, ugly, little things!"

Then, they walk away with the gait that an elephant uses when carrying a basket of children strapped to his back — first one hip then the other, in a combination that would make a horse laugh. They cannot see that my motives have always been for the love of my work.

To the ordinary layman whose idea of Heaven is to be idle, I am simple or just plain crazy. To the intelligentsia, my convictions are attributed to overactive pituitary and thyroid glands. To those who are entirely devoid of high idealism, I am searching for a way to profit through my baby work. Judging solely from the remarks of others, I have been suspected of having a corner on the "market" — as if such a thing existed for children.

"What does she do?" they continue to ask. "Does she provide a ready-made child? Once other souls grow attached to it, does she work them for money?"

Always money, money, money — and never God! It never dawned on them that I might possibly be faithfully serving my Maker without considering my private affairs. Man and money, both movable, changeable, so-called necessities of life. But God always remains the same.

It is the strangest thing, the power of money. I have come to understand the deadening effect to which the jingle of coins have to one's aesthetic senses. Those who have too much money and everything cut and dried for them lose what makes this life worth living. In man's equipment for the busy work-a-day world, there are two necessary evils: 1) the time clock; and 2) the wage system. Together, these factors lead to a misguided sense of what a person is worth.

What is that power that made the dollar sign hideous and obnoxious to me? That power that produced such ecstasy and satisfaction in my work — a craving to serve without a time clock and without remuneration? When one works in that spirit, it is impossible to not achieve happiness. The emphasis is shifted away from the reward obtained for performing a certain amount of work. Rather, it becomes true and easy to proclaim, "I love my work, and I do not expect any reward. Why, I have my Heaven right here on Earth in seeing my babies thrive. My work is inspirational; it is a memorial to my son."

One becomes a target the moment she dares to do something different from the other sheep. I have been called extravagant, with the attendant tang of a 'slur.' To be downright candid, I have been called queer for all my life. On later occasions — by the newspapers, no less — I have been called Lady Bountiful. I considered this an improvement, giving the impression of a Fairy Godmother. I used to take these names in, thinking how little anyone understands the mechanism of the female conundrum. Accepting this criticism amiably — and at the same time observing the tired and miserable people who are bent on diversion — my reply is that I have found my happiness. There must be a method in my madness, and I just keep going. This cold-blooded, mercenary world can stand a single freak like me. My existence must have been intended or I never would have lived it.

I admit that it was an extravagant idea, quite broad in its scope, that compelled me to devote my life to serving humanity. But it only seems this way because our world has become so blinded by confining, man-made laws under which universal love cannot be expressed. I could never escape the irony that degenerates, murderers, crooks, and boot-leggers who operate under such laws are not sought out. Instead, I have been scrutinized for serving humanity. In the demand for me to work under a license that does not exist, my enemies overlooked any good there might be! They consequently undercut a self-appointed servant of God. But of course, that never stopped me.

Out of necessity, I have developed the ability to get hilarious where others might shed tears. This is largely due to the strain that materialists brought upon me in their misinterpretation of my work. When it got to the point where I thought I could no longer stand my position, I turned to the only power that could provide an answer.

"What else would you have me do, God?" I asked.

His answer was instantaneous. "Tell the story to the people who live."

That is precisely what I intend to do in these pages.

"Having mothered, brought up, and found homes for 170 children and babies over the last 15 years, Mrs. Louise Sullivan of Pasadena is going to write a book about the religious and spiritual truths that have come to her throughout her labor of love. It ought to be a book worth reading — that is, if there is anything in my belief that the first requisite for writing a good volume is having something to say."

- Los Angeles Examiner, October 1930

The First Child

Beautiful days do occur in Chicago. This was one of them — June, 1915. As I glanced out of my bedroom window overlooking the velvet lawn, I felt a temptation to pitch my shoes and stockings sky-high and revel in the dew, wiggling my toes in and out of the longer grasses. And when I had used up the dew, I dreamed of lying down on the terrace, facing the endless expanse of filmy clouds and thanking God from the innermost depths of my soul for His many blessings and kindnesses to me. Then, I would rise and resume my work, feeling a new lease on life.

This temptation often turned into a reality before sunrise, though no one in the neighborhood knew about it. It was after experiencing this thrill of the natural world that I first thought of little, barefoot children running on brick pavement with their hair flying in the wind and their voices penetrating the clatter of trains. Would they not love to be turned loose in my yard? How cool, soft, and soothing the grass would feel to those little feet; how they would enjoy some reckless abandon, snatching wildflowers from the perennial gardens. They would spy the chicken yard and let out shrieks of delight that would make the hens forget their mission on earth. The old rooster would cockle-doodle-do, demanding the reason for the commotion.

As I came out of my trance, I asked myself a simple question.

"If not intended for children, what are chickens, flowers, and good-looking lawns good for?"

The answer, of course, was nothing. Getting so excited, I decided to put my thoughts into action. Although my four lovely children were living with me, it had been my dream for ages to have another baby. I had even suggested adopting one, only to hear the stern rejoinder.

"Never mind that adoption stuff. Our own or nothing!"

As for having another biological child, I had been sufficiently warned by my doctor. After having twin babies three times in succession, he assured me that it was suicide to try for another. I knew he was right, but the words were not any less cruel.

The wonderful maternal instinct that had been the outstanding feature of my life was not something to be overlooked. I did not intend to continue without a child or a baby on whom I could shower my motherly love. I quietly asked myself: what did this intense love of babies mean?

While out on a drive, I would watch people, all hustle and bustle, wondering how they got that way. How miserable their drives were, I thought, looking out at the world like a stuffed mummy beside my self-styled "boss." My arms felt so empty, aching with the imaginary loads I wanted to carry.

Now, my husband was just as enthusiastic about automobiles as I was about my home and my children. He always wanted something better, faster, and classier, which led him to order a new machine for a long-discussed trip across the country. I sat in terror as he opened up the muffler, certain that each explosion would land me on top of the Masonic Temple.

It was clearly evident that I was made all wrong when I didn't jump at the opportunity to join him on his trip. But I couldn't bring myself to go with him. All I remembered of other trips was the hustling in and out of towns, always in the dark image of high chandeliers we had left behind. This trip struck me as another wild goose chase. In the end, he motored off to Florida on his own. A farewell honk as he turned the corner at Kenesaw Terrace told me that he was on his way.

The next day was beautiful and sunny, marred only by the absence of a child.

"I am my own boss now," I thought to myself. "I'll have a personal holiday, according to my own ideas."

Suiting my action to the thought, I called Kenzie. Soon,

we were headed in the direction of the nursery. Kenzie tried to dissuade me, well-aware of how my husband would react.

"You know, Mother — you gave him enough when you handed us four to him for a wedding present!"

"I know that," I replied. "But I am not going to keep them. As soon as I hear him returning, I will take the children back. There can't be any crime in wanting to give some children a change."

I had never been inside the gate of the day nursery. Not knowing a soul, I introduced myself, apologized for intruding, and told the matron what I had in mind. Though she was very pleasant and friendly, she imparted that the children all had mothers who called for them in the evening. As she spoke, I spied a pale, hollow-eyed youngster standing in a corner all alone. Drawing the matron's attention to him, she told me his story.

"Oh, yes — he is quite sick. He has just come from the County Hospital, recovering from measles. He really has no business being here, but his mother has to work."

"Do you suppose she would care if I took him home? Do you think she would let me?"

"Well, she might, but I didn't think you wanted a sick child."

"He looks so sad and forlorn. It makes my heart ache to look at him, and I couldn't forget him. Please, let me take him, won't you? Tell her anything you want; tell her that I will pay her weekly if she will only let me have him. Maybe I could get him well, and he would have such a wonderful time. We have a great big yard with a fence around it, and he couldn't get hurt. Go on, please let me take him. It is terrible to leave him alone like this all day, standing over there on one foot like a sick chicken."

That little boy needed a mother, and I just longed to pick him up. However, I realized her difficult position and could hardly believe my ears when she answered me.

"All right. I will let you."

"Now, be sure to tell her that I love little children," I said. "Tell her that I will be good to him and make him happy. And please try to make her feel that I have honest intentions. She can trust me."

With these instructions, I gathered up my precious bundle of lanky, two-year-old legs and carried him out to the car. Kenzie, who had been expecting me to come out with a bunch of wild hooligans, couldn't believe his eyes.

"Why mother, I thought you wanted some children to play in the yard. To hear them laugh and watch them have tea parties with the little dishes that you played with when you were a little girl."

This is what I had talked about on our way to the nursery, but this frail bit of humanity had shifted my state of mind.

"Well, I did," I answered. "But this little thing has been sick and needs a mother more than the others. Maybe I can get him strong before the traveler returns. Why, you don't know how happy I am. Wasn't it wonderful of that matron to let me have him? I left the phone number for his mother to call me, and I won't know whether I can keep him until I speak with her this evening. I hope she will let me."

By this time, I had wrapped the auto blanket around the little one to keep him from the wind of the treacherous old lake.

"Well Mother, you certainly have a queer idea of a holiday. But I tell you, we better get him back home."

That's one thing we agreed upon heartily. As Kenzie walked through the door of our home, little did I dream of what changes were soon to take place. Kenzie walked straight up to my room and laid the little boy on my bed.

"Who is he?" the butler asked. "Where did you get him? How long are you going to keep him?"

"Bring me some vegetable soup, whole wheat bread, and milk," I replied. "And don't ask so many questions. He is here, and if his mother will let him stay, I will keep him until my husband returns."

I'll never forget how happy I was to feed that little thing. Holding him on my lap and giving him little mouthfuls was a thrill to me. After he finished a good first meal, I hugged and kissed him.

"Call me 'Mother,'" I whispered in his little ear.

"Mother," he repeated. I will never forget that voice. It seemed even more wonderful than any 'Mother' I had heard, and yet I worshipped my own babies.

I couldn't understand myself. Why did I feel so light and

airy, as though I had wings? I was so busy and content all afternoon, and I never thought of being tired. While the little one was napping, I got out some regular baby clothes to see if I could make them fit. Once I was finished, I quietly snuck into the room and stood beside his bed. I was thrilled beyond words at the fullness of a child in my care, if only for a short time. Feeling my motherly love upon him, his little eyes opened.

"Want up."

"All right, darling. Mother's going to dress you and we are going out for a walk. I have the cutest baby carriage for you. But first, you must drink your milk."

After squeezing him into one of the biggest baby dresses, I got out my darling little baby pins with the tiniest gold-encrusted daisies on them. My mother had given them to me when my first baby was born. They helped to close the gaps in the front, and then the crowning glory: a bonnet! I will admit that it looked queer, and the little fellow knew it. He looked at me with such a strange expression, as if to say "the rest of it is nice, so I guess I will have to stand this silly stuff."

After getting him all togged up, I carried him downstairs. Think of me doing that when only twenty-four hours before I could hardly crawl down alone.

Now, I commenced to strap the little one into our brand-new baby carriage. There is a saga behind that wonderful contraption, which had serendipitously been delivered to our house just a month before the child came into my life. I was not expecting to care for a baby when I bought the thing. I had spent an hour looking at the different models before I finally decided on the one I wanted.

"I am buying this for one of those life-sized baby dolls," I told the sales clerk. "Haven't you seen them in the toy department? They are just darling."

"You don't mean to tell me that you are spending all this money for just a doll."

"Sure, why not?"

I left her there — utterly dazed — and walked through the store as one in dreamland. As I wound my way through the lineup of beautifully groomed cars on Washington Street, I spied my husband waiting for his freak wife. All of a sudden, that baby carriage loomed up as big as a house. Just as quickly, my wits came to my rescue.

"You ought to see what I bought Isobel for her birthday," I blurted out with all the confidence in the world. Isobel was his weak spot in my foursome, and I hit the nail on the head. By the time we pulled into our driveway, I had aroused his curiosity to such an extent that he begged to know what on earth I could have bought that would require a truck to deliver! Meanwhile, I was quaking because I had Isobel to face. I tried to get her enthused over what I called her birthday present. When the cat was finally let out of the bag, I can't say that she was particularly keen to receive a baby's carriage.

Don't anyone think for one moment that my preparation

was just foolish extravagance. I thought if I could get the family used to seeing paraphernalia around the house, it would be easy to slip in a baby a little later. Women are not so dumb after all, eh?

After walking with the child, I sat on the veranda. You can imagine how much I trembled as the hour approached when the boy's mother would phone me. The thought of parting with him after such a short period of time was almost too much to bear. Exactly as our old grandfather clock struck six o'clock, I approached the ringing phone. Fearing to lift the receiver from its hook, I prepared a couple of bribes on the tip of my tongue. To my delight, however, none were necessary! Just like the matron, she consented to me keeping the child.

We agreed that the boy's mother would call the following Sunday afternoon, which gave me a few more days to mother him. With the correct food, baths, naps, and a surplus of love, he couldn't help but thrive. What a wonderful satisfaction it is to care for a child. They respond to whatever treatment one gives them, and the results show in their little faces and their eyes: the windows to their wonderful little souls.

I certainly remember how I felt the next Sunday before the little one's mother came to visit. I was cold, clammy, nervous, and afraid that I might not meet her expectations. After the boy's nap, I got him all dolled up, placing him in his carriage and buying him in lace pillows. Finally, noticing the same woman pass the house twice within a short space of time, I walked towards the entrance and called out.

"Are you looking for a child?"

"Oh, are you Mrs. Sullivan"?

"Yes. Come in and take a look at your baby."

The woman was clearly startled to see the boy so changed. She could scarcely realize that he was the same sick boy she had left in the day nursery.

"My, he is a lucky boy to have found you." She paused before resuming her speech.

"Why, David — you don't look the same at all to Mama. You look like an angel baby. What's this nice lady doing to you? David, don't you know me? Don't you remember Mama? Don't you remember that I used to bring candy to you?"

"No no," I butted in. "I don't think he has forgotten you. It's perfectly natural for everything to be so new and strange to him. Don't feel badly; he'll forget me as soon as you take him away, though I dread to think of that day. You know what I wish? I wish you would let me keep him for three weeks, and you could visit each Sunday. You wouldn't have the expense or the worry, and I'd be in my seventh heaven playing mother to him. We would be glad to have you spend Sundays with us, and that would be a holiday for you, too. What do you think?"

The woman looked me straight in the eye.

"Why would you be bothered with him? With these beautiful surroundings and servants to do everything for you, I suppose you only get the good part of looking after a child."

"You surely don't understand," I responded. "Why, I

wouldn't let anyone touch him but myself! No one has laid a finger on him since he came into my home. I do everything for him. That's the reason I want him. I look forward to putting him in his bath and sprinkling talcum powder all over him. I get the most wonderful thrill as I snuggle him up in a bath towel. He brings me back to the days when my children were babies. They always seemed to me like gifts from God."

"I still do not understand you."

"No one does," I replied. "And I would not be surprised if they never do. My older brother says I remind him of a canary in a gilded cage, flapping my wings and breaking them in an attempt to get out. I do not like to sit in a Pierce Arrow, all alone. And every time I drive downtown and hear the clang of elevated cars, it reminds me of prison doors. I know I am funny, but we are all made differently and this is my idea of being happy."

As I discoursed on my peculiarities, Kenzie called from across the veranda that he and his chum Al were going out for a drive and would be back a little later.

"Would you like to go, Mother?"

"No, I am visiting with David's mother."

The woman looked inquiringly at me.

"That's Kenzie," I told her. "He drove me to the nursery the day I picked up David."

"What does he think of someone else's child living in his home?"

"He doesn't care. He knows that I am happy and that I love children."

"He certainly is a fine-looking boy. So tall and manly — what a wonderful smile he has."

As she spoke, Kenzie became even more dear to me. I thought about how he had helped to get the little fellow, even though it was all against his better judgment.

David's mother was relieved to know she had no worries as far as her son was concerned. She left with the understanding that he would stay with me until my husband returned.

After ten days of motherly love, David was running around with a wonderful improvement in him. At night, I asked myself: why had I not gone on that motor trip? What made me see plainly those messenger boys in their blue uniforms, trying to catch us? Why the depression of leaving my grown children behind? Why the happy relieved feeling to stay at home with them? I noticed all these things, but couldn't account for them. Thus, my days of happiness and sunshine continued.

My Dear Kenzie

Every afternoon Kenzie would take us for a drive. This afternoon in particular, we had a special objective. We were to visit our doctor, who was also a friend of Kenzie's. When we arrived at the rendezvous, Kenzie looked back at me before greeting his friend.

"Mother, I never saw you with such a wonderful expression. You should always have a baby in your arms."

"I wish I could; I'd love to." And I drew David a little closer to me.

I sat there in silence, completely engrossed in such an intense love that I will never be able to explain or adequately describe. With this silent adoration consuming me, and without warning of any kind or premeditation, I pierced the ether. For appearing directly over Kenzie's head, I beheld what was to me a Vision of Jesus. Immediately, I spoke to the Vision in my mind.

"Oh, God, please give me all the little babies I want. I'd be willing to do anything. I would even part with the son I already have."

And as I mentally said the last word, the Vision disappeared and I suddenly dropped back to earth. I settled back into my corner, held my baby closer to me. Tears were in my eyes.

I never mentioned what happened that afternoon to anyone. That Spiritual experience was sacred, too sacred to even want an explanation. Having no knowledge of the Bible, not knowing anyone who did, and living so much within myself, I said nothing. Sacred things are never discussed, but I pondered deep in my soul. Being absolutely oblivious to all things round about me, all I sensed was vast illumination over the head of my seventeen-year-old son. Ever after on my mind was stamped indelibly that wonderful expression, filled with pity and sorrow and sympathetic understanding, surmounted by divine love. Radiating, scintillating brightness. All else seemed in utter darkness, but I was not. In my arms was the Reflection from the Light that forever makes dark corners bright. God's recognition of unselfish service to humanity.

Thus fortified, I was able to disregard man's attempt to stop God's work. What was even more wonderful, I was filled with such confidence and fearlessness that I did not hesitate to attempt anything, no matter how hopeless from the other person's viewpoint. In my mind I was serving God, not man, and with that understanding based upon my faith, I carried out my work.

After we got home, Kenzie went out to see his rabbits and chickens. Like all boys, he was either raising or selling them. Many a time he would come to me and bemoan his fate.

"Isn't it too bad, Mother? Guess I had the incubator too hot. Look Mother, they were just ready to be hatched."

And there would be one hundred or more little dead chicks! That is sufficient to dishearten anyone. This time though, hanging from his left hand, was a big white rabbit, his pet. Together we had been paying special attention to her.

"What is the matter Kenzie? She is so limp."

"I don't know Mother, but a dog must have managed to get inside the pen while we were gone."

Holding its pretty, white head, he showed me where she had been bitten.

"Now David won't have his little bunnies." And that big boy stood there with tears in his eyes because his mama-to-be rabbit had been killed. It depressed us both, but I came to his rescue.

"Forget it," I said. "It's only a rabbit. You can get another one and buy some bunnies already made. Just be thankful it is not you nor David. That would be something worthwhile wasting your energy over."

"I can't just forget about her. She was as frisky as anything when I fed her this morning. And now she is dead." Taken by his words, I hastened to prepare for the inevitable conversation.

"Come Kenzie, let's sit on the veranda. There is no such thing as Death, anyway. I dare say the bunny right this minute is having a better time than we are."

"Don't you believe Mother, that when you die, that is the end?"

"No," I responded. "And I'll tell you why. When I was about nine years old, my chum passed away very suddenly. Her poor mother cried terribly. One day, she asked me to go to pick my mother's clematis vine so she could string it around her daughter's picture. I can still remember the thrill of picking the long-trailing, sweet-scented vines. 'That's more like it,' I said to myself. 'Keep her out in the open with live flowers around her' And I knew that out in the grove, she was not dead. Her very spirit was alive. Now, that's my childhood recollection, and while it is no proof, it is indicative of something."

Seeing that he was still engrossed in what seemed to him irreparable loss, I shifted my angle.

"Years after your Grandmother died, she appeared to me three nights in succession, each time saying the same thing. At first, I thought it a dream, but when it occurred the third time, I followed her advice and was successful. The feat was nothing short of a miracle. It proved that she was not dead — her memory was not the least defective, her interest in children was still intact, and her mind was able to operate."

But still, my Kenzie was not satisfied.

"You were too young to remember when little Thornton was taken away," I told my son. "I was only twenty-five years old. It seemed as though God were inside of me, attempting to comfort me. In spite of my sorrow, I felt an exhilaration I could not understand. It was Thornton's spiritual presence. When a minister came to console me, I surprised him by saying that I felt God was there with me and my baby. I told him that I believed there is no death. And he smiled at me, and responded that he was pleased with my understanding."

Now, I could tell that I had captured Kenzie's interest, and I ventured further.

"I have shown you the little box on my closet shelf with Thornton's ashes. I have even opened it. It took me weeks to do it, even though I grew cold every time I went near that part of my closet. Every time I opened it, I had to use a trunk to help to discipline myself, I always put that box in with my clothes. If you can only make yourself look at it in the right way; you see, it is ridiculous. You might just as well hang on to a lot of expired insurance policies, then adding up the amounts feel all puffed up to see how rich you are, when in reality they are not worth the paper they are written on. Their day of value has passed. Just so with our bodies, Kenzie. Just a little house, which when the all-powerful hand of God sees fit to vacate that wonderful invisible soul; that connecting link with God, just floats on, never to die. Then the little house, no matter how beautiful, is no longer needed.

Take it from me, Kenzie — don't you dare waste money on a grand funeral because I would certainly laugh."'

"Mother, undertakers and florists would certainly choke you. You would put them out of business."

"Perhaps they deserve such a fate. The undertaker comes onto a scene with a level business head, intent on selling his products to mourners who are overcome with grief. If people insist on spending money when a so-called death occurs, why not use it to help starving people to live? Why send money to foreign missions to educate the heathen when your own country is swamped?"

"Do you believe all this stuff you have been telling me?"

"I know them in my heart. You better remember what I say, in case you are unceremoniously cut adrift from your mother. Train yourself along these lines, Kenzie."

And with that, I gave my son a kiss and sent him off.

An Unspeakable Loss

THE NEXT NIGHT, I ALLOWED KENZIE TO GO TO Riverview, an amusement park. I was so happy that he asked for permission, mentally comparing him to other boys whose Mothers never knew where they were.

The morning after Riverview, he called me to his room and told me he had been awake all night with a sore throat.

"Why didn't you call me?" I asked.

"I didn't want to bother you, I knew you were busy with David all day, and that you would be worried."

The Doctor not being able to come just then, Kenzie got out of bed and drove to his office. When he returned, I happened to be standing at the head of the stairs and noticed how he seemed only able to drag one foot after the other. He said he couldn't help it, on account of how dizzy he was.

Isobel returned later with a report that Kenzie had that

dread disease: black diphtheria. His room soon had the appearance of a hospital. Nurses and health officers came, and demanded us to quarantine. Then Kenzie told me I'd better stay out of the room.

"David isn't very strong, Mother. He might get it and die."

That darling boy, even thinking of everyone else in all his suffering. He was the considerate type though, who said little and smiled much. The kind of a boy everyone likes.

We all spoke with hushed voices and walked with soft footsteps. There was a sleeping porch off his room, and I would go there to speak to Kenzie through the open window. He was too sick to answer. The Doctor came many times each day, and I soon discovered that Kenzie's friend, whom he had gone to see, had passed beyond.

A couple of days later a great ship called "The Eastland" capsized in the Chicago River, throwing mostly women and children in the water. Hundreds drowned. The very air seemed fraught with death. I remember going to the window later and telling him about the tragedy that had befallen The Eastland. Kenzie seemed interested, but the nurse cautioned me afterward not to mention such things, and I wondered why. With death all around me and with him so sick, part of my heart was filled with an intense faith in God; the other with agonizing torture. How wonderful God is, and how merciful, to keep hidden from His children, the very things that would make us unable to venture forth another day.

What a wonderful relief it was to hear the Doctor finally

announce that Kenzie was through the worst of it. I even snuck into his room and discussed a fishing trip he wanted to take. How happy it made me to see the little smile come into his eyes.

The next day, the travelers returned home. When they finally walked through the front door, there was David to meet them: the little fellow that I was supposed to send back as soon as the auto rounded the corner.

Dan and David got quite chummy, which tickled me. After supper that evening, I sneaked in to see Kenzie.

"How does he like David?" Kenzie asked. " What did he say about his being here?"

"Well, he must like him, because he let him eat nearly all of his chocolate ice cream, and he let his watch strike for him."

I was referring to Dan's Swiss watch, which strikes the hours, minutes, and seconds and sounds like the tinkle of a tiny bell. Kenzie smiled at me, acknowledging what I had gotten away with.

The next morning, the rest of the family was inoculated. Everything seemed serene but in my heart, there was a terrible ache. How thankful I would be when I would really see Kenzie up and out once more. Kenzie gave a hurried call for gruel, then a hot foot bath. With all of these tasks, I was not suspicious. It is the only time in my life when I was so completely in the dark. I had not the faintest idea of what I was facing.

After the gruel was sipped, Kenzie told me he was tired and wanted to sleep. I left the room and started dressing David with a feeling of calm. A few minutes later, the doctor followed me into the hallway. His face paled as soon as he inspected my son.

"Kenzie is having a race with death."

"What do you mean?" I asked incredulously. Why did I not understand? The boy whom I worshipped was sinking, and I couldn't grasp the import of those words. Was it possible that the same wonderful hand that guided me later on was deadening my senses? Was He preparing me to meet the blow that would come when I returned to the room and watched my son's last spark leave his body?

"Oh, Doctor!"

"Now, don't cry, don't make the slightest sound, for Kenzie can still hear you. You will worry him."

I waited outside the room in terrible anticipation, numb to the world around me. Finally, the doctor came out with a grave look on his face.

"You have something wonderful to keep before you," he told me. "Your son died with your name upon his lips. 'Mother is a good Mother,' he told me. 'A good M-O-T-H-E-R.'"

I stood speechless, not making a single sound. When I walked into Kenzie's room, I could not believe what lay before me. Just a sweet, smiling countenance; not a trace of his intense suffering. All I could hear was 'Mother is a good Mother. A good Mother.'

From that instant, it became my watch word. Something to live for; something to prove. After the Doctor had left, in spite of his warning, I quietly entered the room and stood right beside Kenzie. I felt guilty before him, but not before God. I bent over and kissed his darling forehead; then cut a lock of his wavy, mouse-colored hair and placed it in a handkerchief."

"Please God," I prayed. "Help him; help me. He has suffered so much already. Please God, my life in return. Just keep me busy and don't let me look back. That's all I ask."

As I gently closed the door, just crying dry tears inwardly, what was it I heard? As though God were sufficiently close to whisper in my ear.

"Fear not, I am with you... "

I had the peculiar feeling that I could go through anything, as long as God could keep me from looking backwards. With a strange feeling of spiritual uplift that anesthetized my heartache beyond explanation, I closed the door forever on the peacefully sleeping form.

When my child breathed his last, I immediately connected it with what I had offered just a few weeks earlier.

"Oh, God," I had told the Vision. "Please give me all the little babies I want. I'd be willing to do anything. I would even part with the son I already have."

It became my sincere belief that my offer was accepted.

My child was taken as a sacrifice for a lifetime of baby work. It was as though I stood between two fires: my God and my child. Then also, what right had I to dispose of my child's life? After he was taken, the feeling came over me to offer mine, which I did.

I could not alter what had occurred. The Rock Foundation for this life was laid that day, and having no alternative, I placed my life in the hands of God, willing to go wherever He directed me. My only request, and which I continually repeated, "Please keep me busy and don't let me look back."

The Eastland disaster made it almost impossible to get any attention. We had to go out of our neighborhood to get a minister, who delivered a very short funeral service. While the minister was praying, I felt Kenzie with me. I felt that it was worrying him to see me suffer, so I tried to be brave. I knew he always worried if he thought I was unhappy, so I contained myself, thinking of him as living, but just out of my exact reach. It all seemed like a dream. If I managed to control myself, I thought I could feel him near me.

Within two hours, all that was mortal of my child was turned to ashes. In the late afternoon of the same day, I was handed a box.

"What is this?" I asked.

"Kenzie's remains."

Trying to be brave, I took the box and placed it on the shelf beside the other one. At that moment, I had the intuitive knowledge that this life would be well-lived.

My father, arriving from Cincinnati in the late afternoon, was completely overcome when he learned everything had taken place early in the morning. I couldn't cry and I had to comfort him. He could not understand my composure.

That night when he was retiring, his door partly open, I saw him sitting on the foot of the bed, sobbing as though his heart would break.

While sitting with him, as though I were looking through a kaleidoscope, I saw myself beside babies and children. It was a glimpse into the future, just a bit of encouragement. God was encouraging me, lifting the veil to provide a panoramic view at a brighter future.

"What can I do?" I asked God. "How can I help him? He was so young, but God you know he was a good boy. Please let me take up his work. I won't stop day or night God, if you will only let me. Show me what to do, please."

I do not know how, but the days passed. Each night, I rocked David before putting him in bed. I never rocked a baby, but a wonderful sense of calm enveloped me when I held that little thing in my arms. I felt a lightness of heart, as though God and Kenzie were right there with me.

A New Purpose

As soon as the quarantine was lifted, I went back to the nursery. Each day, I returned with a new set of children. Such a mad pace was kept up for two steady months. For August and September, all I did was bathe, feed, undress, sleep, and dress six to eight children each day. That same porch where I had talked to Kenzie through the open window now held all these dear little children. My boy was gone, but in his place were some of God's numberless poor. With each breath that I drew, I thanked God for making it possible for me to substitute life for "so-called" death. Instead of a feeling of desperation, I had the wonderful, contented feeling that I was helping humanity. Instead of that heavy, dragged out feeling, I was buoyant. I really could not understand, because I knew I loved my own child.

Standing in the doorway opposite Kenzie's room, I would

look over my flock of different colored top knots, all sleeping, all comfortable, all clean — perhaps for the first time in their lives. It reminded of a Sunday School card that my teacher had given me with the Good Shepherd watching over His flock. In his arms, He held a lost sheep that had gone astray, reflecting how God didn't worry for the "Ninety and Nine" that were together, but for the one that was lost. I applied this to my baby work and felt a wonderful thrill administering care to the unwanted baby, the unattractive one.

After they awakened from their naps, I would dress them. Their clothes were so tattered and torn that I couldn't bear to put them back on at the end of the day. I sent the little ones home with a paper parcel containing their belongings. On their bodies, they wore the sweet scent of talcum powder and fresh clothing that they deserved.

Two months of this, and as I would return from the nursery, I would find myself yearning for a baby! These were only children. Just think of it, still wanting to go on! No one understood how I could keep up the perpetual motion. I hardly sat down. My meals I ate on the "fly." That intense yearning was as though I had never had a child near me; and I knew the weather would soon be chilly and we couldn't continue the trips downtown. The wind was signaling the approach of winter and the children wouldn't be allowed to come on the cold drive to my house.

I remember how empty the car seemed as soon as I had to part with "my children" for the day. However, I felt content at having stuffed them with enough nourishment to keep them from growing hungry before the next morning, even if they didn't have anything but water. Returning from the nursery, I would remind myself of a turtle — just pulling my head under my collar and thinking how I might manage to keep busy during the winter, longing for a baby.

I learned a great deal from these experiences — one of the main things being that it takes a wonderful unselfish quality for a mother to separate herself from her child, because she sees a better future for it elsewhere. That's the reason I loved every mother of every baby that was given to me. Each mother worked under the immutable law of God, which is the Law of Love. This, in turn, precluded the possibility of trouble returning to me. After all, it is impossible for trouble of any kind to arise when Love is the governing force. We all know that God is love, and God presided over my babies.

Soon, my dear friend Reverend Norman B. Barr, called to check on me.

"I didn't know you had a child so young," he said upon seeing David.

"Well, he isn't my child, Mr. Barr, but the little boy Kenzie and I took from the day nursery to give him a holiday. And then you know, Kenzie was taken and David is still here."

"Are you interested in such work?"

"I have always loved babies and children; I'd be glad to do anything in connection with children."

"I'll give you a card with the names and addresses of several children I know. Some are orphans, some are half orphans, and some are worse than either."

Even now I feel the thrill those words gave me! Just think of being able to get into the heart of suffering humanity without even an effort on my part. Just a willingness, and God was making the rest possible. The minister did not know my interpretation of this life — of the Vision I had had — but that did not prevent his thoughts from dovetailing into my spiritual experiences.

Giving me his card and starting out the next morning, we drove to some of the addresses. It was clear by the poor condition of the houses that the families were in the most trying of circumstances.

"I have heard you are in need of child care," I said after knocking on one of the doors. "Is this the case?"

"Yes. He is in that shed back there."

The steps were so rickety that I thought each one would precipitate me to the filthy ground beneath. I opened what was just like a stable door. Anyone less anxious would have turned back, but I was all the more happy to help anything in that hole. It was so dark, with no windows — just the light coming in from the opening. I stretched forward, not leaving the top step to go inside, so terrible and black looking, but there was the darling, helpless baby. He couldn't have been a day more than six months old. Sunken, hollow eyes; death like pallor; dirty, hanging on for dear life to a ginger ale bottle half-filled with coffee — cold, grayish looking, sloppy coffee. Just think: a baby — their own flesh and blood — and they let me take him without saying goodbye or knowing who I was.

With the most wonderful feeling of contentment, I was eager to get home. This little thing was almost starved to death. The first thing I did was give the poor baby a bath. Then out came my baby clothes, which I wrapped around the little body. My better half didn't care, he wanted me to forget my sorrow. But he couldn't have dreamed of my insatiable love for babies. Babies came and children went and I never stopped. Instead of getting weaker, I got stronger. The more I did, the more I wanted to do. Words fail to describe my happiness with another baby in my arms, and half a dozen children all mine to sleep under my roof, for me to wash, dress and feed. Wasn't God wonderful to me?

Eventually, I took the baby home. The mother never dreamed he could be so pretty. She wasn't the only one — everyone wondered at the change that would come over the babies that I mothered in such a short time. They could not understand. I did, though.

I could always feel that outpouring stream of love that was being continually replenished and which my little babies eagerly drained, in consequence of which they thrived. Such happiness, such rapturous joy out of such sickening sorrow — and all because I love to serve, rather than to be served. If only I had the power to make others understand, there would not be one unhappy person in the world. It is so easy. One little move out of your regular path, with a simple desire to help someone, and something is bound to happen. Keep on the alert and listen for signals. They come just as distinctly as the bells "sound" when the "wigwag" warns of an approaching train. Take any old thing and love it unselfishly and watch the result.

I never waited for Sunday to worship. It was going on all the time. I worshipped when I placed a bottle of food in each dear little mouth and conducted my rounds to prevent anyone from getting wind instead of food. I worshipped when I tucked twelve babies in at night. I worshipped when I accepted a new little baby in the morning and had to get up especially early to get the others bathed, fed and back to bed again. Well, any mother knows what I mean when she has a dozen babies to handle, and I wanted to have everything ship-shape so as to have complete isolation with my latest addition. Just to be alone with a new baby. Each one was more wonderful to me than the one before.

Kenzie's Nursery: The Center of My Home

❦

JUST THINK — THEY WERE ALL MY BABIES, ENTRUSTED TO my care. Not thrown at me nor haggled over, but given to me in the same spirit that I was privileged by God to carry on my work. That is the only reason that I never got tired. My love continually increased, and with each baby I was better fitted for what the material mind could only see, a terrific undertaking.

That said, they truly belonged to other people. I was just helping them to get started. In some cases, it took three years before the parents wanted to accept the responsibility of taking them back in. In that span, the atmosphere of my forty-foot bedroom changed completely. When my family began to increase, springing up overnight like mushrooms, I had to expand my workspace. All the servants were moved to their original quarters over the garage, and I took over the upper floor. This consisted of five rooms and a bath — all of which took on the aspect of purity. White, painted walls, white enameled furniture, and white linoleum inlaid with a small black figure covered the entire floor. For the different rooms, I ordered different sized beds for the different sized babies. I allowed no one on this floor, not even to clean. As I mopped, dusted, and fired things down the laundry chute, I worshipped. This became my Sanctuary. I endeavored to keep the solemn promise made to Almighty God. As such, I christened the space with the name of my son.

"The McKenzie Lowndes Memorial Nursery"

It seemed a perfectly natural thing for me to do. Just as well, I made a number of little banners out of royal purple satin and gold script:

"With my own hands."

"Mother is a good mother."

Kenzie's last words were a reminder of my goal and what I wanted to prove. Undoubtedly the appropriate song was, "Onward Christian Soldier," which I found myself humming many times.

There was something very peaceful and soothing about that room, and I craved to be alone in it with just my babies. As plainly as I ever saw my child while here on this earth plane was I aware of his Spiritual presence, and overlooking all of us was Our Heavenly Father, which as if by magic placed me in a veritable Garden of Eden. I was a changed woman, filled with such rapturous joy every minute I breathed that it was impossible to tire me.

There was a large, tiled bath that I turned into a cafeteria, and over which I became "chief cook and bottle washer." The curtained shower was ideal for the electric stove, which I placed on the top of a very high magazine stand. All the shelves underneath came in handy for "what nots." Lined up against one side of the wall were ten nursery chairs, all working. During the performance one evening, one of my "in-laws" intruded and thought it such a unique sight. He couldn't believe so many little babies could be made so comfortable, look so happy and content, under such requirements.

Only on very special occasions was anyone allowed to enter the Nursery. One little girl whom I had mothered longer than usual was like a watchdog. My son-in-law had occasion to discover it. Attempting to let some of his friends have a peek at my babies, she planted herself in the different doorways.

"Don't you dare put your foot inside; Mother does not want people near her babies."

"She is well-trained," my son-in-law later remarked, and so I made an exception.

The babies in my nursery never had the black-and-blue marks that were so common in fancy daycares that were equipped with manmade licenses. One of my children — a three-year-old — had 23 of the blackest bruises on his spine from waist to neck. How did he get them? He had been beaten by his guardian because he was homesick for his mother. Think of an adult beating a child of three years old, just because he cried or wet the bed. These are the people who flourished under a license.

You see, then, why I am so averse to the system. I am convinced my way is the only way to work. With God in mind, children are not mistreated; the extra work is not noticed. With God in mind, ones' work becomes a pleasure. In serving God, the almighty dollar is not the object.

My nursery was always filled with boy babies and girl babies, pink nighties and blue nighties, trimmed with rick-rack. I shocked a saleslady at Carson Pirie's by ordering six dozen all at one clip. That was all that they had, and I wanted my babies to be alike and exclusive. One of the only material business-like things that I ever did came as the result of that order. She told me I was entitled to a discount if I purchased in wholesale quantities. I wondered just what my inquisitor would think. I could not give him a definite line-up. How could I? All I knew was that I was going to need loads of baby clothes because I had room in my heart for loads of babies, and God was going to give them to me. Womanlike, I always loved pretty clothes, but my most memorable heartthrobs along that line were experienced in the baby department.

In my nursery, I was like a giraffe — my feet firmly planted on terra firma, carrying out the practical side of this privileged life. While I craned my neck endeavoring to get over the top, my thoughts explored celestial realms. One does not find many people in this material age who can remain on one track uncommercialized for a length of time, but I certainly did. Nothing could move me from my thoughts of babies and God. The laundering of 'my babies' clothes was no small item. It kept one woman busy six days out of every week. Then, those baskets of dainty hand-made clothes were put in the sewing room, each article to be inspected by a woman who added the missing buttons and lived up to the adage "A stitch in time saves nine." When every baby was dressed and laid in its little bed for a peaceful sleep, I could say "Amen" with a degree of satisfaction.

I could never have retained my poise had not my work been based on love, on service. Had I started on a business plan, with the accumulation of riches and my goal, and showed the same energy, the same intensity of purpose, I would have become unstable. Working for money, with the energy I was given, would have been a tearing down process; but working with the love of God and humanity, my very platform precluded the possibility of permanent drain. I had not an ache nor a pain in my body. My heart was so full of love and a willingness to serve that the string of babies in front of me did not mean work. Rather, they were food for my hungry heart and prevented me from having one idle moment in which to retrospect.

This uncommercialized life with "my babies" was not lived to tell you how to wash, feed and dress babies. They were given to me to satisfy a great love, and this humanitarian service proved a veritable hot-bed for soul development, which made it possible to pick up messages via my Spiritual Radio. Who talks over that Radio? Not the dead, I assure you. They are the so-called dead — but more alive than the inhabitants of this earth plane. I know whereof I speak!

The Mother of a Community Mother

PERHAPS AT THIS POINT IN THE TELLING OF MY STORY you would find it interesting to know how a person with my ideals came into existence. My mother was a diminutive type of French ancestry, and I was the bane of her existence. She taught me an original system of adages when I was so young that I did not understand their meaning. Phrases like "make your word as good as your bond" puzzled me in my childhood, but I have lived and learned. My poor mother — she had to deal with me trying to climb telegraph poles to get higher than any of the boys. No wonder she had nervous dyspepsia. She always brought the same threat.

"Just wait, until your father comes — I'll tell him." He repeated a rather unsatisfying response to her.

"If she doesn't do anything worse than that, she'll be alright."

Now, in my baby work, I always visualized myself as a hollowed pumpkin lantern with an ever increasing desire to fill it with Knowledge of God. Perhaps that was because my mother always said that I was as dumb as a beetle or just half-baked. Her special form of entertainment was to take me onto her lap, and while rocking sing the following chant:

"Lulu is our dumbest girl, dumbest girl, dumbest girl."

After a couple of repeats came the Grande Finale:

"Dumb the live-long day."

When I got older, I was always told to help the sickly because I was half-baked, and helping others was the only thing I could do properly. One day, coming in late for dinner, I got a severe scolding from my mother. I had been helping old Tom, a man of our neighborhood, mop up his face on the street corner.

"What do you mean by hanging around a drunken man?"

"Who said so?"

"Your brother saw you wiping his face. Why didn't you come straight home?"

"Haven't you told me dozens of times to be sure to help sick people?" I asked in utter disgust. "He was sick."

"He was drunk, you dummy. Haven't you got one ounce of just plain common horse sense?"

"Isn't a drunk man a sick man?"

And at sixty years of age, I still think that I was right.

Another time, I got "in Dutch" for literally carrying out what I heard. My Mother loved flowers, and they always

47

rewarded her efforts by blooming profusely. Springtime in the suburbs of Cincinnati was heaven on earth to her. She loved watching the crocuses and hyacinths break through the earth after a warm gentle rain.

But our next door neighbor had chickens, and the male owners were important as they belonged to my Daddy's Saturday Night Poker Club. The game was really an excuse to store away lager in their bellies. Anyways, the chickens would go roaming into my mother's garden, and Daddy wouldn't say a thing to his friends.

"I wish to Heaven that somebody would kill all those chickens!" my mother would cry. "Every single leaf is eaten!"

And then would follow a spell of vomiting from nervous dyspepsia. It was no wonder aided by her smelling rotten cigar stumps and secondhand beer.

At this time, cousin Chuck was living with us. After one of her explosions, while she was busy at one of those foot treadle sewing machines, I approached him. Her expostulations were still ringing in my ears: "Those devilish chickens!"

"Mama says she wishes somebody would kill those chickens," I told Chuck.

So, we hid in the strawberry patch until a perfect beauty came strutting up — a grand old rooster, "The Cock of the Walk." I don't know how I managed, but I caught him by one foot and gave him a good yank until I had hold of both.

"Chuck, you hold his head and I'll twist!"

And it worked! He was kilt! We did this to two successfully, but the third one was especially hard to knock out. He put up a terrible fight, and above the screeching and squawking, my Mother's soprano voice came from the serving room.

"What on earth is the matter with those chickens? I never heard such an infernal racket!"

"Don't make so much noise yourself," I called back. "We got two killed and the third one is breathing his last."

"What do you mean?"

"Didn't you say that you wished somebody would kill all of them?"

Did I get a scolding! Perhaps you will think that I was a cruel child, but understand the mind of a young one who wants to please her parents! I did not understand what I was doing; I only wanted to earn the pride and good will of my mother. The result was her hardened opinion that I was half-baked. That helped to make an introvert out of me. I was told that anyone able to talk on just one subject was an ignoramus. So you can see how my relationship with God was cultivated. He was the only one to whom I could talk and feel sure of not getting the gong!

As a child, I had a penchant for getting myself dirty. Boy, would Mother get angry for giving birth to such a good-for-nothing tom-boy.

"Did you do your patchwork, or any of the dozen and one things that you should know how to do? What on earth are you ever to amount to — always singing and whistling? Don't you know that a whistling girl and a crowing hen always come to some bad end? And why don't you play with your dolls, instead of always being with the boys? God help your children if you ever have any. They'll starve to death and go naked." And then she would vomit.

"Just you wait until I have my own," I thought to myself.

By this time, she would leave me in the bath with a cake of Ivory soap. In the silence, I would talk to God. I would ask him to give me a child one day, and I would pretend I was nursing it. After an unearthly long time, my mother would shout at me from the kitchen.

"What on earth are you doing in there?"

If I had been as old then as I am now, I would have answered that I was talking to God. But being a tom-boy in my youth, I responded that I was counting the black and blue marks on my legs.

"There are ninety-six on my right leg, and I only got up to sixty-five on my left one. Now I have to start all over again as I forgot the spot where I left off!"

If I could make people think that a baby was mine, I was in heaven. At the age of thirteen, my mother's friend asked me to mother her baby while she and her husband went to town. I walked miles across town to take up the joys of being a young mother. When I got there, they were ready to leave, and I was in my element. The act of holding God's image cheek to cheek filled me with a thrill I had never yet experienced.

Well, I was going alone nicely, proud as a peacock, and

tickled to death. Every time I'd see someone coming, I'd stop and take a look at my baby. Then loud enough for them to hear, I'd shout, "That's a good baby. Mama's little darling, keep on sleeping."

I'd wonder if I had fooled them, and on I'd go.

I had just passed The Altenheim on Burnet Avenue, a great open sweep of land, when leaves and dust began to flurry and scurry. As they got stronger, a terror seized me. The wind had a knack for developing into near twisters without warning, and that is precisely what happened. The carriage handle was pulled away from me, and the baby rolled out. My heart stood still, my eyes blinded and stinging with dust.

While I picked up the baby, a bunch of hoodlum boys nabbed the baby's afghan and made off with it. I thought I might get scolded for that, but I could stand it because the baby was not even crying. I hurried along. The wind subsided, and then it began to rain "cats and dogs."

Close to the railroad tracks, I ventured to the back door of a cottage to escape the elements. Gently and timidly knocking, a very kindly lady let me come in, carriage and all. Once the storm passed, she gave me a pat on the back and helped me out with the carriage.

"You are going to be a good little mother someday," she said. If only my mother could have heard her.

Well, there the parents were, anxiously awaiting my return. Unbeknownst to me, the trip to town had been called off as soon as the storm had started, so they had been on tender hooks a long time. When I turned in on the steep winding walk leading to the house, pushing what looked like an old-fashioned four poster bed on wheels, for the first time in my life I was a heroine.

Outside of relying upon God, I was as independent as a hog on ice. When I first married, I was very young. I had long been building my wedding finery: six darling Empress Josephine tea gowns with Watteau plaits in the back and long trains bedecked with lace and ribbon. All swishy, lovely bits of femininity. My heart beat fast and extra strong at the idea of wearing these gowns — why? Because that meant I could be a mother! My own maternal figure, though, did not understand. What she focused on in my dresser were disclosed baby clothes — all sweet-scented with sachet powder and tagged with blue ribbons.

"You better wait to have a child until you are married," she said sarcastically. This puzzled me, as I did not know how the whole process worked!

And so you can see that my mother bred much pain in me. She also awakened my passion, which served as an inspiration to me throughout my dozen years of baby work.

The Babies Who Needed Me Most

As I dove deeper into my work, I wondered if a family friend — a doctor who worked in a hospital — might be able to connect me with more little ones in need. Sure enough, he imparted over dinner that his work brought him in touch with babies who needed care. So, the following Sunday I visited his hospital.

I was interested not in the babies who looked well, but in the hollow-eyed ones with high cheekbones, sucking on thin, bony fingers. There they lay from the beginning of the month to the end, that is if they lived that long. But with so much red tape, taking them in was an absolute impossibility. I might just as well have wished the building to crumble and expect to see it do so, as to get my hands on one of those helpless babies.

As we passed into another group, I saw a bed upon which

a little child was dying. It wouldn't be long now, and yet not a soul near it. I stood there spellbound, while no one else seemed to think it worthwhile. Just an ordinary, everyday occurrence. Men and women and children dying every minute. The same circumstances surrounding the individual case. Friendless, father and motherless. I couldn't feel that way though. I felt we are all brothers and sisters, and God the Father of us all. That little child was as much mine as if I had given birth to it. When life was ebbing, I felt it was my duty to remain by the side of that little child who was so soon to be acquainted with "Our Father."

With many persons around in their spic and span uniforms, that tiny little baby was left alone to die. As I stood there, that life flickered out, and I thought how strange that I couldn't have that baby. I would have held onto it until it passed on. It wouldn't have been left alone. I collected my senses, and I am not exaggerating when I say I reeled out onto the sidewalk and had to stand against the car to keep from falling. My legs were weak under me, and everything swam before me. That enormous white building that held so many little lives that I felt I could have saved, and I was powerless to help even one.

Why was I made so? No one else felt the way I did. Why did that Sunday continually haunt me? Today, twelve years after, I can still see those thin, yellow faces that could have been changed to pink, smiling baby faces.

In the presence of Death, I feel the departing soul is but a connecting link. God is waiting, and my message of love is being carried to Him. Death loses its terror when understood in its true meaning. Whether Heaven or Hell has predominated is optional with the individual Dreamer.

It was this experience that pushed me to seek out babies with the worst problems imaginable — likely due to improper care of the mothers before birth. On one occasion, I received a call about a baby's perpetual cries, which were putting the parents in a fit. The father jumped as a frog does at red flannel when I suggested that the baby join my family. Within the hour, I was traveling toward 72nd Street to pick up the child.

The morning was bitterly cold — the wind off the lake was howling through the baby carriage. I wondered why the contents were not frozen stiff when I stuck the new member of my little family in the bath. Placing him flat upon his back and gently throwing the water over him, my hand sliding down on his tummy, I realized what the problem was.

"No wonder he cries all the time," I said to myself. "He is ruptured." I had no book learning or formal knowledge, but God directed the diagnosis into my mind within two minutes of the baby's bath.

Immediately, I called the mother by phone.

"Did you know the baby is ruptured? Has the doctor seen him?"

"Yes, almost every day."

"Has he seen him naked?"

"Yes, he has examined him thoroughly."

"Well, that seems funny. As far as I can make out he has a terrible gap."

She became very excited, but I told her to calm herself. I was not afraid, but I did want her to know right off the reel so she would not suspect me of harming the child. Sending for a doctor, it was found to be a correct diagnosis and the little fellow fell heir to a cute little corset, which he wore for many months.

In the end, the boy experienced a full recovery and I was deemed a miracle worker. The truth, however, is that I did nothing but listen to the Hand that was guiding me. With regular hours, lots of love, plenty of fresh air, and correct food, my inner knowledge and belief in God enabled me to work through any hardship.

In one stage of my career as a Universal Mother, without any warning, four babies became deathly ill. I was not so concerned about two of them as their own mothers were in my home and could see for themselves what the outcome was each day. The way one mother expressed herself each morning, "Gee, doesn't she look terrible. I wouldn't be surprised if they all passed out before night."

And the servant of God talked to Him in this way: "I'm not afraid to tackle this alone. All that I ask you to do, God, is to keep all their friends away from me until they are all well."

That was some feat, and it was performed successfully — as if God could ever fail. The babies continued to vomit for days on end, and their eyes dropped way back into sockets, deeply outlined with that indelible blue tint. But they recovered, and my faith in God was even more strengthened.

Another one of my little babies was one that never stopped crying from the day it was born. It was about three months old when I was directed to its mother. If I had lost my way, the yell would surely have enabled me to walk directly to it, even had I been blindfolded. The incessant cries came from pain, with the poor creature having abscessed ears since birth. The baby's history would scare anyone if the noise did not.

Oddly, the little one immediately stopped crying when I accepted it into my arms. This event naturally encouraged the mother to release the child to my care. She was not the only one who felt this way. Every mother was glad to give me the sickly, unattractive baby that cried from A.M. to P.M. and all through the night. It is worth noting that this lack of crying was a theme throughout my baby work. Not once did I have a baby with colic, not one accident of any kind. How do you account for it? Superhuman? No. Just a human being who believed implicitly in God, and who must have been born with the necessary ingredients. When opportunity knocked at her door, and having the courage of her own convictions, she was a human who laid down her life willingly.

One day I was asked to see an especially sick baby. It was so emaciated that I was even warned. Of course, they were only planting a seed of courage, hoping it might develop sufficiently within me, to undertake the task that was before me. After getting my other babies to sleep, and with my heart pounding with excitement, I jumped into the machine and soon arrived at a tumbled-down tenement.

The young man who was driving me lifted one end of the blanket, took a look at the child, and uttered an exclamation of horror. I sat with the lowliest baby that had ever been entrusted to me with the happiest thanksgiving in my heart that I had ever experienced. To think that God would trust me sufficiently, to place that almost lifeless form in my care. That tiny bit of humanity, repulsive to everyone but me, had two missions on earth, as you will later see.

We hurried home. The only thing covering the baby's nakedness was a blood-spattered cotton cloth, which I had to leave on the little thing until it soaked off in the tepid water that I ran in my bath. Throwing a blanket on the bottom to insure its protection and comfort, I gently placed that inde-scribable piece of humanity, with its little hard, bony skull, in the palm of my left hand. While I was swishing the water back and forth over its long skeleton, I heard a sob over my right shoulder. It was my own father, who was visiting me at the time.

"Why are you crying?" I asked him.

"Don't you think you are undertaking too much?" he answered. "She may die in the bath."

I told him I was not afraid. Something too wonderful was going on inside of me — something so overpowering that I felt my only relief would be to turn inside out. It was a bursting sensation, with love pouring into me in such quantities and filling me with fearlessness. I could feel myself crying inside. I cannot say whether from joy or sorrow: joy at my privilege of caring for her; or sorrow because she needed that care. So intense and so intermingled were my feelings, that I could not tell where one began and the other ended.

Just as though God were right there with me, talking to me from my innermost depths as I knelt beside this little flickering life, I heard a distinct voice.

"Do this. You do this for me."

"God," I answered, "I will do anything for you. Anything that you will let me do. I love you. Just keep me busy, God. That's all I ask."

There lay that little mortal, almost inhuman figure. Big eyes, dropped way back into skull-high cheekbones; skin loosely covering a foundation of bones, like the mousquetaire gloves we used to wear; raw and bleeding tongue from sucking on a so-called pacifier. She was so hungry. Nearly-starved. Blood streaked the water, and the little nails on her hands and feet had grown through the flesh at a lack of care. The little one had scarcely been touched in her nine months of life, and she weighed only four pounds.

That tiny mite lived and thrived. Inside of two days, her expression changed completely. Her body was healed and her little raw mouth ceased to be a source of irritation. Everyone marvelled. I bought her beautiful clothes. Nothing, to me, seemed too good for her or too much to do. To me, she was as though a little Christ Child had come to my door. Every time I touched her I would get the most wonderful thrill, as though an electric current had swept through my entire body. I would put her into her little bed and linger beside her, so happy to see her cheeks beginning to fill out and a tiny speck of color in the center of each.

Only God knows how I worshipped, and whom I was worshiping. These wonderful moments in my life are the sacred ones that I was selected to experience. When I realized what was intended of me, I did not falter. I feel that I have carried out my privileged duty, and my feelings are my only guide.

This little babe had never been named, having every evidence of not being long for this earth. Realizing what that baby meant to me, I proudly carried her to the Altar where her name was bestowed upon her — the family conferring the honor of naming their baby upon me.

I wanted to adopt the baby, but protests came from both families. Meeting the mother in the church, it struck me as strange to be in complete charge of the baby while knowing that I was only a temporary mother. There was no jealousy — just a sincere thankfulness for the part I was privileged to play.

The child's parents were so thrilled with their now good-looking baby that I was privileged with three of their children, all at one time. The second youngest child had a peculiar way of walking, stamping her bony little legs to emphasize the points she endeavored to make. They all called me Mother, no matter how long or short their visit. It seemed an easy solution to what was really puzzling everyone, as the world did not understand the motive of my work. But to me, it was not a puzzle. I was in the infant stages of my expression of Universal Motherhood.

When Reverend Barr discovered the wonderful change in the little girl, he kindly invited me to attend the annual dinner of the Olivet Institute in Chicago. My tendency was to back out of anything of a social nature, but this being somewhat different, I accepted to show my appreciation for the interest displayed in my work. After the dinner we adjourned to another room where we were entertained with stereopticon views showing the progress of The Settlement. Among the pictures were those of the baby and myself, first showing how she looked when I took her in at four pounds, and then showing how she looked at a healthy sixteen pounds four months later.

They all applauded, which was quite nice to see. But the recognition did not seem to affect me personally. All that mattered was that the baby was happy and healthy. All who are listening — I implore you to live above your own surroundings. Create your own atmosphere, being of the people but not with them.

Each opportunity I had to administer to a sick child was as if God was allowing me to care for Him. Whenever I received a phone call that a mother had just died, leaving a half-hour old baby, I felt an impossible mixture of sorrow, joy, and thankfulness that I had been called. And so you can see why I simply could not give up my baby work. Now just how would one suggest spending my afternoons without my babies? Join one of those card clubs and smoke like an old chimney? It's easy to visualize a large gathering of women playing cards, and little cliques forming, each talking against the other. Think of a whole lifetime frivolously spent. I am always reminded that there is to be a last day somehow or other, when it will be too late to rectify. When one is ushered into the Presence of Almighty God, think of having not one thing to offer Him; just a bunch of score cards!

A Pair of Outcasts

I HAVE ENCOUNTERED SOME CHILDREN CONSIDERED outcasts just because they were born out of wedlock, or because they come from a foreign faith. These babies deserved special care, as I seemed to be the only one in the world who would care for them. A particular example occurred when a woman offered me her unborn baby. At the time, I couldn't imagine it — giving up a little one without knowing what it might look like. Of course, I obliged the woman's request. Seven months later, the same woman entered my door with the telltale bundle and in her right arm. She handed it over to me like a sack of flour, and I took it.

The little boy became so commanding and efficient that I dubbed him "Judge." At the time, he created a little extra excitement in my life.

"Is he illegitimate?" I remember being asked. I was up in arms at the question.

"There is no such thing on the face of the earth. Everything is legitimate if it is made in the image of God. You call a special kind of light and fluffy fudge 'divinity,' but you overlook that spark in your baby."

"Oh, I understand what you mean."

"I am not sure you do," I responded. "Have you ever thought how terrible it is to stigmatize that helpless bit of humanity who can never live it down? Have you ever tried to mother a child whose life was one inextricable question? Have you ever looked into the hunted, bloodshot eyes of a boy, who wonders who his father is?"

Needless to say, my opponents were surprised at my outburst. Hopefully it prevented them from looking upon a child with prejudice, based on the status of a marriage license.

After three years of care and devotion, I managed to locate the mother of Judge. I did not expect her to take the boy, but she surprised me. With tears in her eyes, she accepted him back into her life.

On another occasion, I met a woman who was utterly distraught.

"Please," she cried, "help me. My husband is very sick and I have just come from the hospital with my newborn child. She is eleven days old and I don't know what to do. Our Papa is also quite sick and I got a wire this morning to come at once. I can't make the trip with two children — yes, I have two now: Bobbie and the newborn. I was telling my troubles to a woman this morning and she gave me your house number. She said she was keeping it because she might have to fall back on you one day. If you will lend me only twenty-five dollars and keep care of my newborn for me, I'll make the trip and get him as soon as our Papa is strong!"

"You do not need to lie to me," I said. "Do you want to rid yourself of this child?"

"Oh no. She is the apple of her father's eye. We will come back for him."

And so sealing this token of my love for God, I took the human bundle and hit terra firma. My first look at her, and I nicknamed her Rebecca — Becky for short. Soon after I took Rebecca under my wing, we prepared for our usual winter in Florida. I had five "just walking" babies to care for, but the newborn made the work more than double. As per usual, with my big babies in bed at night, I'd sit before the open fireplace with my "dessert" upon my lap. As I loosened her clothes and let her little legs stretch out toward the heat, those dear little pink toes and highly polished nails spoke volumes to me.

It was not long before I learned that the baby had Jewish blood in her. This made no difference to me. When holding dear little Becky's supple body, a feeling of love spread around the little spaces and crevices around my heart. I was immediately devoted to her. In the eyes of God, we are all alike. We are one and the same, just one big family. I cannot pretend that I did not wonder, watching little Rebecca, if she would one day develop a taste for gefilte fish and matzoh. Or if she would celebrate Yom Kippur. But why let thoughts like these enter? They did not matter. All babies are permitted to thrive under God's love. And so you can see that there was more in my brain than Quick Quaker Oats and vegetable soup.

One evening, I tucked little Rebecca in for the night. Not a thing looked wrong with her, and she fell asleep calmly. But at four in the morning, I felt a gentle tug at my heartstring and was reminded to go to her. Without a cry, her little arms extended as though in anticipation of someone waiting for her. And then she was gone, without any warning to me. Words cannot explain what overcame me as my husband made a big log fire. Just a few short hours before, I had watched her little legs squirm, and now I was preparing for her burial. But along with this sadness, I felt a thankfulness for God. He had shown me that in His sight, we are all alike: Jew and Gentile.

I carried little Rebecca down to the dock, slipped a spray of Baby's Breath into the folds of her blanket, and gave a silent prayer. The neighbors spotted us and later asked us what we were doing at such an hour.

"Her Father has taken her home," I replied. And they never knew that she had passed on. Being a Jewish baby, mothered by a Protestant, and buried under their Rites of the Catholic Church should tell a story to all of us.

Lotus and George

A WOMAN CAME TO MY DOOR ONE MORNING SAYING SHE
had read about my work and was hoping that I would take her
little girl, who was nearly three years old. It wasn't long before
she was one of "my babies." The dear little thing told me how
she was sent to the saloon "To wush the gwowler." She
explained that meant getting whiskey for Mama. That they
always made her sleep on the outside of the bed, and sometimes pushed her on the floor "when they'd get dwunk."

Her father had passed on, so I was more than thankful
that the mother had sufficient maternal instinct to realize she
wasn't treating her daughter suitably. My new little one
became accustomed to better surroundings, and soon when I
was preparing a baby for its bath, she would run ahead and
hide her paraphernalia so I wouldn't use her things for the
"dirty" baby environment!

My new baby went to our Florida cottage many times and had all the advantages home-life could do for her. Never once did I think of possession, although she grew to be very attractive. My object was to improve her for her own benefit, and while I loved her, I had to be very strict, as some of her bad habits were so ingrained. She soon developed into a regular little mother. She'd watch me in my work and hand me things as I needed them, and we grew to be just like "Me and My Shadow."

The mother was now in a sanitarium. I visited many times, and words failed to express her happiness and thankfulness to realize that her daughter was still with me. It surprised her, as she had only counted on me keeping her a month. But I could not bear to part with the little one. I always figured the longer she was with me, the better prepared she would be if someone adopted her.

I kept that little thing for nearly five years and then gave her to a couple past middle age who just worshipped her. The other couple was more than thankful for giving her to them. But I didn't feel entitled to thanks. In my mind I was serving God, and my success was keeping everyone happy by working, leaving no time for retrospection.

When this adoption took place, I planned to visit the mother to let her know her daughter had found a permanent home. She had three other little girls, and I bought Easter outfits for them to cheer their spirits and put a little happiness in their mother's heart. But when I called the sanitarium, I learned that the mother had passed on.

All women inclined as bargain hunters will understand what's meant when I say I took babies "as is." One, the tiniest little mortal had the largest China-blue eyes, enhanced and protected by long, dark,curling lashes. With close-fitting, shell-like ears and a little fringe of yellow silk curls all over her little head, she was the picture of dainty femininity. I called her Lotus.

She did, however, have a very difficult time eating. Her food would come out of her nose as fast as it went into her little mouth, and after one feeding her dress would be sopping wet, no matter how thick the bib. Poor little darling. One day, a woman came in to watch me go through my feeding routine with the little one. I came into the room carrying a big bath towel and a piece of oiled silk with a tiny hole in it, which I slipped over the nipple to prevent leakage. Then, I got a flap fitted into the roof of the baby's mouth, and of course, the nipple was on the under-side. As soon as she tasted the food, she went after it like greased lightning, forming a suction, which kept the oiled silk in place.

"What do you have to do all that for?" the woman asked.

"She has a hole in the top of her mouth and she strangles because the food comes out of her nose."

"Why, that's surely a cleft palate. You must go to Dr. Brophy's office, for he can give you a patented nipple for such cases.

This was my introduction to a wonderful man who could substitute a ceiling in a helpless mortal's mouth until old enough to be operable. So you see how God works. He showed me what to do, sending the right woman to my door with the information I needed. To my way of thinking, this is a very good example of one hundred percent cooperation between God and man.

To show you how I went out of my way to find work and how I was directed, I often turned to the Personal Ad section of the Los Angeles Times for mothers in need. One day, I found a peculiar entry titled, "Mother's milk wanted."

I wrote to her, telling her I had fed many babies, and had been the means of saving their lives. When the woman responded, I learned that her baby was so ill it had to be carried on a pillow. The parents were even afraid of the motion of the car, so I drove to her house, where I saw a terribly sick baby in the yard. The mother understood that it needed plenty of fresh air, and she was seeing to it that it got it.

I told her that if she didn't take it to a doctor before morning she would not have to bother, as I saw the stamp of death on that baby. The woman nodded, and I left.

Later, the grandmother phoned to thank me.

"For what?" I asked.

"For the way you spoke to her; you spoke with such authority — we could never influence her. All along we have realized the baby's dangerous condition, but she was so stubborn. But within two hours after you left, she was on her way to the hospital."

Again I will repeat that I never felt that I personally accomplished anything. The baby recovered, and that severed our connection. That is all I wanted to do: just help. Now then, who helped me? Who printed death across that baby's forehead that made me speak "with authority?" I can only say that it was injected into me when I had my first Vision of Jesus.

On another occasion, I was approached by a couple who needed help with their son, George. He was certainly emaciated, resembling a little old monkey. He had apparently never smiled since his birth. The minute I looked at him, I was pretty sure I'd be able to help him if he stayed with me. Of course, that meant the couple would go home to an empty house with no baby cries — just unwelcome quiet.

It's a funny thing, but men always trust me. When I suggested leaving the baby with me, the Daddy answered at once:

"It's alright with me." I turned to the mother.

"How about you?"

They looked at each other; then I told them to think it over. We had telephone communication, and they could reach me any minute. Like thousands of other babies, this one just needed maternal instinct, a God-given gift. So the couple walked out to the curbing and with their heads together, decided to leave the baby with me.

I took little George, gave him a bath, and fed him my formula — Quick Quaker Oats! He ate vigorously and heartily. I put him in his little bed, and he slept quietly for three hours. When he finally woke, he started playing with his toes, good as gold, with a broad grin from one ear to the other. There was my reward right there. Not a jeweled crown in heaven; I was in heaven all the time.

When the mother came in the afternoon, she could hardly believe it was her own child. His expression had changed and his little cheeks even showed signs of filling out. His eyes were bright and snappy, and he was content.

Occupancy Overload

At the beginning of my baby work, I established a limit of having fourteen babies at once. That number kept me very comfortably occupied and made me very methodical. I reminded myself of a factory hand doing piece work. I had developed a certain way of doing each thing, honed by years of continual repetition that made me speedy as well as efficient. It is really marvelous what one can do with the wonderful body God has given each of us, teeming and abounding with mystery. But despite my decades of service, I still experienced the ecstatic bliss at the end of each night in knowing that I was doing what God wanted. And I was ready to start all over again, oftentimes without ever having closed my eyes.

It was during this time that a timid voice found its way

over my phone. I could tell that the woman was distraught, on account of her sniffling.

"Are you crying?"

"Yes, Ma'm. I don't know what to do. I can't go home with my baby. Mama and I want so much to keep her, but we live in such a small town and we could never stand the gossip. My sweetheart was killed in a train wreck. We were just going to be married. The terrible part of the whole thing is I can never again be a mother. The doctor found it necessary to operate. I'd be so happy if you would only take her. Mama is here with me and she says to tell you that if you got one peek at her, you would never be able to refuse. She's so fat, her skin is like peaches and cream, and she has the most adorable head of red curls, and the biggest bluest eyes, and she most never cries."

Then, she fell into a fit of tears. It took me a full minute to calm the new mother down to the point where her hearing would not be defective.

"Listen, I have to work fast, because my husband has not gone downtown yet. His Roadster is in the driveway. Don't show up until it is gone. Then come to the front door — I'll be waiting for you."

And that is how fifteen babies became my limit. I cannot tell you how many times, nor how long I mothered that number. God certainly put up a wonderful bunch of machinery in my mechanism. Conceit? No, I call it appreciation and recognition of my wonderful Maker. God does not do things halfway. He implanted the ideals and supplied the energy with which to carry them on to completion.

A few days after this increase, my husband happened to come into the bathroom when I had a tubful of babies, all kicking and splashing with their eyes riveted on me. There was my newest addition — the little redhead.

"How come?" my husband asked me.

"Oh, you mean Little Carrots? Why, I've always had her."

He began to count. "I thought we had decided that Fourteen would be your limit. I don't want you to kill yourself."

"Well, Danny Boy — this will be my new limit, I promise you."

No more Titian beauties happened along just at that time, which kept me on the good side of my better half. At least to some extent. With a row of babies before me, they were like a string of firecrackers. One Mastermind set the others off to a laugh, a giggle, or a wee little wiggle. My angelic cherubs could even be ferocious at times. You might be inclined to think their special diet was raw beef — the blood-thirsty way in which they tackle one another. Of course, their wildness wasn't premeditated — even when they set the house on fire! They had piled wicker waste baskets filled with papers directly under long curtains that adorned the floor. Luckily, I was able to douse the thing before the walls turned to ashes.

"I did not make the fire," one of the little boys said "Woosh did it!"

'Woosh,' I knew, was little Ruth.

"You big storyteller!" she shouted. "I just piled up the baskets."

"Well, you set it on fire, Woosh, you know you did."

I understood that they were just children, and that they did not know what they were doing. But such frights certainly did keep me on my toes at all times.

This was not the only naughtiness I experienced. Once, they pitched all of my silver toilet articles out of the window and onto the front lawn. For what reason, nobody knew — they just did. Another time, they locked themselves in the bathroom where they undertook to clean each labeled bottle! They explained that the items now looked cleaner, and if we had not been gifted with a keen sense of smell, we would not have known whether we were using iodine or tincture of myrrh as a mouthwash! I experienced a million other trying experiences that every mother runs up against. But try as hard as I can, I cannot recall ever intimating that my children should be placed in a reform school. Just what kind of a mother would I be? Not what I was destined to be — A Universal Mother and a Messenger — a bridge between the so-called dead and the supposed to be living.

It will be clear to you that I was not always comfortable in my motherhood. On many occasions, I operated out of fear and uncertainty. Once, when I had placed John and Alice in the bath, Alice's stomach started to swell. Soon it looked like an automobile tire, on the point of bursting if one more tiny speck of air were pumped into it. I was petrified to see her eyes staring and glassy, as though she were going into convulsions.

"God, please help me!"

There flashed before me the picture of Jesus sitting in a boat on a troubled sea, rebuking the sailors for their lack of faith. As the waves receded, so did Alice's stomach regain its normal size. And so, by making use of the same faith that Jesus had, I was rewarded.

On another occasion, I was in the bathroom with several of the babies in the bath when something inside of me told me to go into the other room. There was only one baby, eleven days old on that bed. It had just been given to me the day before, and can you imagine my surprise and horror when I saw it hanging over the side of the bed, head downward. In a few more seconds, it would have been on the floor. As naturally as you would say "thank you" to someone you saw, I thanked God for calling me to rescue that baby.

Though it was exhausting work, I was always grateful that I chose a type of labor where the stock is always replenished. There is no danger of it running out, as occurs with butter or eggs in the culinary department. God kept supplying little ones for me. Anything that was motherless and had a beating heart was taken in.

A Bit of Unexpected Publicity

AFTER RETURNING FROM DINNER ONE EVENING, I headed for the kitchen to prepare the bottles for my babies. The phone rang during the process, so I placed the food on the back of the stove while I answered, everyone else having retired.

The man informed me that he had seen the picture of one of my transformed children and proceeded to ask so many questions. I really should have been suspicious, but I was so gullible. To get me to speak, all that anyone had to do was to tell me my babies were wonderful. That is exactly what he did.

Finally, the man thanked me, and I went back to my baby food, having told him all I knew. I soon developed that feeling of being entirely deflated. The only thought left in my entire anatomy was "what a queer time to ask all those questions."

Everything was running smoothly the next morning. Within myself was happiness and sunshine, and I had no care for the weather, people, or what was happening outside. Suddenly, Dave the butler announced the arrival of several men who wanted to see me.

"What on earth do they want with me?"

Dave was almost white. I never saw his old buck tooth stand out so prominently. It wasn't a grin, but a look of terror.

"I haven't a clue," he responded. "What will I do with them?"

"Well, ask who they are and see what they want. I'm not going to leave a sick baby to go downstairs and see a lot of men that I don't even know."

With these orders issued from headquarters, he returned with the astounding news that they were sent from the City Hall to examine the premises.

"If they want to see me," I said, "let them all come up to my bedroom."

Now the City Hall only meant one thing in my life: a big white building taking up an entire city block, surrounded on four sides by politicians looking for an easy way to make a living. As to what these four walls contained, I never gave a thought, aside from the idea that it was something to be avoided.

I looked these men over as they came in, but I didn't budge. I remember thinking to myself that these men had about as much chance of stopping me as if they put a tea-strainer in front of Niagara Falls and then ordered it to stop leaking. But a part of me was dearly afraid. I happened to be standing over a sick baby I had been endeavoring to put life into: a premature baby that should have been in an incubator. He couldn't have weighed more than two and one-half pounds, just as big as a spring chicken. Though I felt like I was drowning, that little one was my anchor. I felt absolutely safe touching that little thing, with scarcely an atom of life.

"Good morning," I said as bravely as I could. "What can I do for you?"

"Well, you see, Madam...that article in the Tribune told about your work. The City Hall wants to see if you are properly equipped to run a hospital."

"What hospital?"

No one knew, but someone had started a report that I was going to have a hospital with a hundred beds. Then, one of my uninvited guests walked over to where I was standing beside this hollow-eyed little waif.

"Aren't you afraid that baby will die on your hands, and you will get sued for all you are worth?" These words caused a feeling of disgust to run through me. What was money compared to that child's life?

"I am not afraid," I told the man. "Nothing will ever happen to me, working with the Spirit I am."

The men proceeded to discuss a variety of modifications to my residence — widening a front stairway, tearing the front door off its hinges. But after inspecting the place, they came to the conclusion that they had been sent out on a false tip.

"These steps are nearly as wide as the City Hall," one of the men exclaimed, as if he were defending me and blaming those with authority. I wouldn't think of mutilating this woman's property. And look how the house is built — it is solid brick. And look where it stands — one hundred and fifty feet from the house on one side, and at least fifty on the other."

By the time they left, all of those men from City Hall had become great allies of mine. It was very evident that they had felt the outstretched Arm of Love and protection that always hovered over me and my babies. Instead of trying to check me, they helped to make it possible for me to continue to scatter sunshine, health, and happiness. As far as they could see, I deserved to look after all the babies I wanted. The surroundings were ideal; and as to my motherly qualities, well — those men would have liked nothing better than to join my nursery. Of course, that is easy to understand. Men are just great big babies and fall for the same tactics.

I always carried the highest possible standard — that of working voluntarily for God's people. All I wanted to do was to care for the most innocent and helpless of all creatures: motherless babies. I did not do this work for monetary gain, but rather to relieve myself of an abnormal supply of love. That was the secret standard I carried. Yet I was held in suspicion.

Thanks to that reporter, my home became a haven of rest for such wanderers. This bout of publicity brought a great deal of attention upon my person and my plans, if I had any. So many darling mothers came to me, I found myself wondering why their own mothers had not hopped into bed and pretended the baby was theirs. The strange part was that I did not have any plans. Just spontaneous combustion and the result; my home, my heart, and my arms thrown open to helpless humanity. Easy for me to understand, but mighty suspicious looking to outsiders.

A Trip to Florida

With the first signs of the approach of another winter — leaves falling and those that managed to hang on changing color — my thoughts were directed to our cottage in Florida. My better half would precede me by a couple of weeks, get all the boats out, and have everything ship-shape in readiness for our arrival. It was quite an undertaking to prepare for such a trip, but when once set, I was eager to go around the world.

Big dunnage bags, overflowing with everything under the sun. It was like a portable dry-goods and drug-store combined. I could have provided for an orphanage if one had suddenly broken loose. By the time the bags were filled, it took all of one's strength to tie it. To lift it was a proposition not to be treated lightly. Think of feeding all those babies on a train. But I knew they would be like little angels.

Being prepared to depart the next day at noon, I received a new call about a little one in need of help.

"Mother," my daughter called out while I was on the line. "You are certainly crazy to take another child. You will just kill yourself!"

But I kept listening to the voice at the other end of the wire, paying no attention to my daughter.

"You see, Mrs. Sullivan," the man on the phone said. "Her people don't understand how to handle her, and the doctor says that unless some intelligent person takes her and makes her use her legs, she will be a cripple for life."

"It's too bad they ever let her get into that condition," I said. "They have taken her from me three times, and the last time I warned them I would not touch her again, because they undo all my work and she is very hard to make thrive. Why don't they listen to me?"

"I know, Mrs. Sullivan, but you see they just don't understand and you are the only one who will take her and not charge for your work, and anyway, you are her Godmother."

At ten o'clock, she was brought to me. She was crippled from her waist down; her long, bony legs completely drawn up, just the same as your arm is when you attempt to reach around your neck. Try it and then you will know what the little thing looked like.

For the trip, it was really a blessing she couldn't walk. Of course she was always recognized as my ugliest baby. But you see with me, Mary coming back into my life reminded me instantaneously of those wonderful words: "Do this. You do this for me." With that simple appeal, I saw the sorrowful, pathetic face before me, so real that I could not close the door. Thus motivated, Mary joined the caravan and we were soon headed for the Dearborn Street Station.

Sitting on the back seat with a string of pillows in front of me, the babies fell sound asleep. With little crippled Mary sitting on my lap, no mortal can know my thankfulness for the part I have been allowed to play on this wonderful stage.

Safely ensconced in the drawing room of the train, I heaved a sigh of relief and let the babies rest. As I opened the door to the outer berth of the train, here were these men offering me their hands, just as though I were on exhibition in a sideshow. It was funny and so unexpected, but they were congratulating me for the nerve and ability to tackle such a handful of all sizes and all ages.

"You are a wonderfully strong woman to be able to travel so soon with such young ones. I must ask, why does your husband stand for all these babies?"

"He doesn't stand, but reclines and lets them crawl all over him."

So you see I had an enjoyable trip; and with all the religion I had in my work, I managed to keep it hidden.

After safely landing at our destination, I found that my husband had purchased a Fifty Foot Raised Deck Cruiser with solid metal prow, for ramming submarines. It was built for the Russian government as a submarine chaser, but it was never used by them. Powered with a Four Hundred H.P. Dusenberg engine that had a top speed of forty-five miles an hour, the boat cut through the water like a flying machine. We arrived at the cottage within two hours.

The house was a dream. Every room had doors that opened out to an exceptionally wide veranda. We had running water and gas in each room, pretty convenient for the backwoods. Each room also opened into the big hall that was our living room, with a big open fireplace. Here we were, water on three sides, nestled up among the trees, and I concocted the idea of calling the cottage, "Babes in the Wood." It was the only material thing in my life that I ever missed, it being such a wonderful background for all of my ideas, and such an ideal life for the babies. A real heaven on earth, where everyone understood, better than any place else, the meaning of my work.

Nothing would have given me greater pleasure, than to have a welfare detective as my guest in Florida. Her suspicions would have been promptly allayed when she became just one more in our thriving colony. Such a glorious life! All the babies who were old enough had their bath in nature's tub that surrounded us. After dressing, each one would be put in a chair before the big open fireplace that was well protected by a screen, with orders "to stay there till Mother finishes with the rest." Then, when all the walking children were ready for their sweaters, I'd throw them in a heap, order a 'huddle,' and let each pick their own, thus teaching them colors. Our special guest, the welfare worker, would have Florida grape-fruit the size of soup plates and sweet as sugar, and all vari-eties of fish pulled from surrounding coves and bayous. We would have given her a taste of night fishing with a headlight on the bow of the boat and using spears instead of fishing poles. Then, when she'd return to California, she'd be forced to acknowledge the wonders of a Florida winter for a three months holiday. Perhaps after this "close-up" of this Universal Mother, she'd forget the old man-made laws that told her to take a tape measure and mark off the space allotted for each bed. She would now realize that there was not a tape measure big enough to measure the love of the volunteer servant of God.

After we returned from Florida, a friend visiting my daughter asked as a special favor to feed Mary. I didn't want to deprive our guest of any pleasure, so I acquiesced. She began at 8:00, and around 10:00 o'clock was still trying to get Mary to swallow her first mouthful. This girl is a timid, little mild-spoken thing who adorns society's drawing room and pours tea with great eclat, but no splash!

"Come on now, my precious Mary," she said. "Eat for me, blessed. That's a good wee girl."

She spoke in a Southern drawl that induces sleep better than any sedative. Seeing her predicament, I offered to relieve her.

"Swallow, Mary," I said firmly. "None of your nonsense. Get busy."

The little drawing room butterfly was shocked. "I didn't think you'd talk to her that way."

"Some of them it is necessary to impress with the fact that you are the boss."

And of course, little Mary took a big swallow. It is this instinct that I know was suffused in me by my Maker. An incredible ability to know how to mother babies who bore no biological relation to my person.

Eventually, Mary's family was ready to take her back in. By the tone of the letters I had been receiving while at the cottage, you would think I had kidnapped her even though they had begged me to take her. That's human nature for you. But here was Mary, able to walk just as straight as any of the other children — little crippled Mary who was so doubled up when I started on that trip. Mary's mother came forward, and Mary, still clinging to me and calling me "Mother."

"Here Mary," I told her. "Here's your real mother; you are going home with her now. Goodbye, darling."

She walked on with her kin to live a happy, fruitful life. Just then, a friend of the family who was staying with us in the cottage felt impelled to comment on the exchange.

"Goodbye?!" he asked, stunned. "Why Louise, is that all there is to it? Don't you get paid for all that work and all that trouble? And besides, the child is now able to walk!"

"Well, isn't that sufficient payment? What better reward could one ask than to know that a little child, who would have sat on her little "BTM" all her life, is able to use her legs and run away now if she feels like it? I'm perfectly satisfied."

"For the love of God, Louise; I never heard of such a thing."

And that man is a perfectly good Catholic who answered the call of the church bell regularly. As we all know, that is quite customary. However, he hit the nail on the head, without realizing it, when he exclaimed, "For the love of God!"

Releasing My Babies

ALL OF MY BABIES WERE PLACED IN MY ARMS BY trusting mothers. From association before birth, she would know I had her welfare at heart and that I was attempting to be a mother to her. Think of these poor outcasts who have all the physical pain, plus the mental torture of knowing it is compulsory to part with their baby. I have so many letters thanking me for the love and kindness extended when their own fathers and mothers had turned against them. Love begets love. And so, it was impossible to keep babies from coming my way.

"Don't you get into trouble," people have asked me over the years, "when mothers want their babies returned?"

How could I? I never took advantage of any mother at any time. My work was a work of love, being carried on as a memorial to my child. Would I besmirch his memory by the tiniest act that would leave doubt in any one's mind? Every mother knew from my actions that I was only extending a helping hand. She was free to come at any time. My mothers understood I had no ulterior motive.

I'll demonstrate by way of example. A hurried ring at the bell one afternoon, which I nearly broke my neck to answer because I was afraid the butler or a member of the family would sidetrack whoever might be there, fearing the visitor might overwork me. I had made them all promise that they would never turn away a woman who wanted to see me personally, but I felt they secretly reserved the right to make an exception to the rule because I "just never knew when to stop."

As I opened the door, I was greeted by the happiest, sweetest smile on the face of a girl.

"Can I have Tommy?" she asked. "We just got married this afternoon and we want him so badly. We are going to move a little way out of the city, and we think everything will be alright sometime."

In the nursery, I set my eyes upon the young woman's little baby. Dressing him in some of my best baby clothes, I placed in her arms what I considered the most wonderful wedding present a queen could receive, even if a little in advance. By this time, she was in tears. Just getting married, I imagine that she was caught up in a whirlwind of excitement.

Perhaps she was wondering, deep in her heart, if I had really meant it when I said she could have him whenever she developed the means to look after him. Inwardly, I was happy and thankful to realize that when put to the test, I could give up the child with a wholehearted feeling.

"Your path might not be strewn entirely with roses," I told the mother. "But you have done the right thing, and God will help you."

I do not mean to suggest that my baby work was void of pain. With every thriving angel, I had to accept the eventual separation that would occur between myself and my new baby. It was as if every day a bird of prey was circling, getting closer and closer until finally carrying away my darling baby. If it is possible for you to realize my heartaches, then think how powerful Almighty God was to keep me from dwelling on it. But think how all-knowing He was to make me forget myself and take care of the next baby. Think how wonderful He was to demonstrate that everything in this world is merely loaned to us — even our children — and that we must forget material possessions to save our souls.

Still, I cannot tell you how difficult it was, parting with the children who I had come to live as my own. It was not easy for them either, in beginning a new life with their parents, or with a pair of foster parents. Take little Michael, for example. A few days after leaving my care, he spied a woman dressed in all white that reminded him of his "Maw-moo" and tried to get off the bus to follow her! When he was put in his bed for a nap, he dreamed of me calling him in his sleep. When he woke, he ran around the house carrying my picture, smearing it with tears. And when his mother attempted to kiss him, he told her that they didn't taste like Mawmoo's kisses. But what could I do? That woman was his mother, and she would be the one to raise him. There is virtue in being hurt so many times. One hopes to gradually become immune to heartache, but that has never occurred for me.

One mistake made in the first year of my baby work comes forcibly to my mind. After transforming a neglected little baby into a beautiful child, I prematurely returned the little one to its mother. Becoming home-sick for a sight of the little fellow, I risked going into the terrible neighborhood where its family lived. And after locating the place, I didn't find the little child. The mother was a widow, and I was dumbfounded to hear a gruff male voice through the doorway.

"She gave the brat away. Don't bother to come back."

From thereon, I learned that I must guard the babies that come under my care, even if they do not legally belong to me. For I was the only loving presence that many of my babies had.

Perhaps you will ask if I ever worried about being exploited by an angry mother. Being an exponent of the immutable law of love explains why I never feared bad results when I took babies in a spirit of love. I gave out nothing but

love and it was impossible for anything but love and its attributes to return to me. I knew the law under which I was
working and every mother felt it. That's the reason I didn't ask
for signatures where I could protect a mother in so doing. In
the law of love, there is no such thing as fear — only Faith —
and that is why I have been successful.

Being Misunderstood

LIFE CERTAINLY IS INTERESTING, BUT THE PEOPLE ARE queer. I dodged them every time I had a chance. What they were trying to do to me, I never took the trouble to find out. All I know is that it was very difficult to convince everyone that I was not a public institution, but a private citizen with a simple desire to save human lives. I wasn't working according to man's idea, namely, salary and a timeclock, but giving unlimited loving service for the benefit of all mankind, expressing Universal Love. What I craved was the association of the human heart and to help humanity wherever I found it possible. I climbed every barrier that got in my way and was thoroughly happy doing what everyone else calls "work." This is the quintessence of soul development.

At times, I was even referred to as a fanatic. The basis they had for that opinion is beyond my understanding. Could a religious zealot mother, bathe, dress, and feed fifteen babies at one time? Could she get them to sleep as if by magic, and not have a sound but contented purrs like little kittens? Think it over. Still, I cannot count the number of times my intentions were questioned. People accused me of selling babies — if you can imagine such a thing. Not once was I given the benefit of a doubt. How do I know? Well, my neighbors who were bombarded with questions about the Freak — that is, the woman who believed in God — told me what the world said about me.

Even my own family misunderstood me. Along my journey, I encountered the time when my own daughter delivered a child of her own. I remember the little thing being handed to me. Here was my first grandchild. She had a wealth of jet-black hair, which was in stark contrast to my daughter's beautiful blonde head. I felt quite nervous handling her, which seems strange with all the newborn babes that I had. Everything was totally different. And never once did I "soar to other heights." I was just thankful that my daughter had her heart's desire.

I puzzled over this for quite some time. Why was I not filled with the same joy that I felt when handling the children in my nursery. What I realized, gradually, was that I craved outcast babies — the babies no one seemed to want. I connected them, in fact, with that Babe who was born many, many years ago in a Manger. Perhaps that explains why I have loved the babies that no one else on earth wanted. My overpowering love for God was trying to find a way to express itself, and I can only describe how certain babies affected me. Something mysterious told me that no matter how many grandchildren I might have, God's little castoff children would somehow always be more grand in my eyes.

At first, my daughter demanded that her child be treated differently from the ones in my nursery. She lived down on the second floor, singled out and very exclusive. There, the little imp got spoiled. Every time the phone rang, she yelped; every time anyone dared to budge, she fanned the air with her tiny fists. The more attention I gave her, the more she demanded. Finally, I expressed myself to my daughter.

"This baby is no better than all the others. They are all equals, and as such they should be together, sleep together, and receive the same treatment."

The ultimatum was calmly accepted. So we moved the little bed upstairs, and by my action I proved the sincerity of my service. I felt happier, and we all slept peacefully thereafter.

One point that I may as well settle right now. I have long been criticized for spreading love to babies to whom I am not related. My family has been upset by this at times, citing that "blood is thicker than water." But what my family had to learn is that I have always preferred water. And what scathing criticism I withstood. When I felt I was at the point of explosion, the misunderstood granny would politely sachet out of the room. And in the privacy of my own chamber, I reflected how eternally thankful I was for the reality of God in my life. With people, it is a case of here today, gone tomorrow. But with God understood and experienced, the family is much broader than one's blood. All of us are part of the same family.

While my children never understood my work, they never tried to prevent me from going on with it. They gradually got used to not expecting me to join them at mealtime. I do think they expected me to slow down once a child of my own flesh and blood arrived. In fact, the opposite occurred — my shop continued at full blast — and I was a bigger puzzle than ever.

The criticism I received never really bothered me because I knew whom I was serving. What did bend my wires was the effect that such talk could have on my babies, once they grew up. Those little ones, who had weathered the storm and been buffeted around did not deserve the stress of hearing that their mother was "well-fixed," or that she "made a good thing out of raising and boarding babies for Hollywood actresses." They did not deserve to hear that I had received a nest egg for taking them on, or that I sold a couple of yearlings at a profit. My babies should know that I took them in for no reason but the love in my heart. And if I need to prove that, I have a wealth of rebuttal evidence at my command.

It is impossible for man, when blinded by the so-called almighty dollar, to get a true insight into anything. Battling all along the line as pioneers are compelled to, it has been proven to me that the best results are attained by strict adherence to God's Law of Love, and not under narrowing and confining man-made laws. Holding fast to God automatically released a great increased surge of joy, which increased my capacity for practical helpfulness. Once I heard the Voice of God and got such good results, together with a wonderful sense of Freedom — well, what man said carried as little weight as rings of smoke.

After being battered by those who misunderstood me, I was always reinvigorated in the silence of night when the babies were sleeping and I was left alone with my thoughts. It was during these hours that I prayed to God. The vitalizing ether pumping into my veins renewed energy, stimulating me, making it possible to draw my loved ones closer to me. I knew God could make Himself heard any time or place if I were in a receptive condition. However, intuitive knowledge made me understand that the right conditions must also be met to feel the Spirit of my child. When the world slept, it was easy to draw Him to me.

Along the lines of little secret nocturnal visits, I always encouraged a midnight bottle. As plain and distinctly as one experiences mental telepathy, on this plane, I would be conscious of Kenzie speaking to me.

"Mother, don't work so hard; I'm alright," he would tell me. And I would go back to bed, thrilled beyond words. No wonder people did not understand how I could lose so much sleep and never feel tired the next day.

Lip service is of little value when love of God is not expressed by practical demonstration for the benefit of humanity. We are plainly told: "But be ye doers of the Word, not hearers, only deceiving yourselves. Not everyone who says "Lord, Lord, enters in." Understanding people with the wonderful interpretation God made possible for me, success was always mine. I gained a wonderful life without a moment to think of myself and a firm conviction that each breath I drew was in service to God.

I encourage you, reader, to pursue such a level of worship and service to humanity. If you disconnect selfishness from your anatomy, the problem is solved. It can even lead to world peace.

Escaping Death

THE WORLD WAR WAS RAGING. EVERYONE WAS DOING their bit, so I tried to go overseas. The only position that was open to me, however, was to supply a unit in France. I was prepared to bring my work to the old continent, but I was not prepared to get mixed up in the business of killing. I do not believe in War. And so, I remained in America.

My better half had not wanderlusted in some time, so off he went. The coast was now clear, so my nursery filled up automatically. With a husband off my hands, I amassed thirteen babies. After a few months of this bliss, I was called to the phone. My husband wanted to meet me in New York; I was to hop on a train immediately. But I could not, and I felt guilty. The week before this, I had noticed that the eyes of one of my babies was very bleary. His nose was running, but he ran no temperature. A little girl had the same symptoms, along with a grayish, spotted looking throat.

"Diphtheria, my dear child," the doctor reported. That was all he said. With such a contagious diagnosis, every servant left. The health officer came first and placed a placard for everyone to keep their distance. The babies had to be inoculated. Any mother knowing what work it is to attend to one baby — try to figure how to prick the delicate, sensitive skin of thirteen babies. But I didn't get panic stricken. I had faith that I was made strong enough to stand it.

I called the hospitals, but all seemed to be filled. The few that had the space refused to accept babies from my care.

"Well, who are you anyway?" they asked.

"I am just a mother, and I love babies. I am doing this work as a memorial, and I don't charge."

"If you haven't a license, we can't recognize you."

By this time the disease was well established. Only God could keep me going. Luckily, my daughter Isobel had a friend who was an intern in the County Hospital. Knowing the nature of my work, she sent an ambulance who would take the two little ones to the Durant Hospital, which specializes in infectious diseases. No one could understand my heartache in sending my babies away in their hour of most need. No one understood how I loved them, how I fed them, and how I covered them at night.

Finally, the blankets were wrapped around them, and they were put on the stretchers with their dear little faces only visible. They begged with their eyes not to be taken from me, but I knew it had to be done.

Soon, my better half returned home. I thought he might be afraid to enter the house, but he did not care. The only thing that seemed to worry him was whether the doctor would be able to find a spot to inoculate him. Everyone was happy. They talked about the war, and they talked about the Armistice. I stuck to my babies.

My baby Donald, about fourteen months old, and Katherine, five, were progressing. The attack was light, and in six weeks, I was able to bring them home. Little did I dream when I brought Donald from the hospital that we were so soon to be permanently separated. I was out in the yard playing with him when a woman phoned about adopting a baby boy. In a few moments, a car eased along the curb. Taking Donald's hand, I walked out to the car to say "Hello." They began to rave over his beautiful curly hair and wonderful physique. One thing led to another, and little Donald had a permanent home. Years after, a man called to tell me what a wonderful boy my baby had developed into. Give to the world the best that you have and the best will come back to you.

One of my babies was particularly difficult to place in a home, as the doctors advised of a medical condition that was not apparent to me. With this news, I expressed a desire to adopt her immediately. A sick baby needs a mother more than a well baby, and I took her in for another six years. Eventually, I found her mother who had not laid eyes on her since the day I had assumed responsibility — when the little one was eleven days old — and she went back to her own mother with my name.

During my time with this child, I cemented a bond beyond my wildest imagination. Her hair was almost black, with a copper tinge, and her big, brown eyes pierced me like a dagger. According to the doctors, her condition would keep her from ever walking or talking. But one day, at the age of three, she looked at me and clearly said, "Bye Bye." Then not another sound for six months. And then, to my shock, she began to sing! She loved "Marchita" — following it over the radio and getting the change in key perfectly. "Mighty like a Rose" was another of her favorites. Her little voice had such a musical ring, it would seem God had purposely kept it sealed to create a reward for those lucky enough to hear it. Her repertoire of Sunday School songs was even more extensive. Soon, she was tripping through the house, singing at the top of her voice.

Can you blame me, then, for listening to what God says over the advice of doctors? He was the one who performed this miracle. His Echo never lost its ring, nor the import of it: "Do this. You do this for me."

It is true to say that the skill that God instilled in me translated to adults, as well as children. Once, an acquaintance who was staying with me fell deathly ill with heart and kidney complications. When I checked on her, she was sitting bolt-upright in bed, gasping for her breath. Not wishing to disturb a doctor at that early hour, but in great agony and distress, a wave of compassion and sympathy came over me. Leisurely, I slipped into a chair. Without a book in hand or the utterance of a prayer on my lips, I sent her a surge of that most wonderful something that I directed towards my babies. Immediately, her shoulders drooped and she gradually eased into a more comfortable position in which she could breathe comfortably.

"Louise, what did you do to me?" she asked in the morning. "I have never felt such wonderful relief. I was in such agony until you came in."

"I did nothing. It was God."

"There was something definite coming from you to me. I felt it. It was like a strong current and was so heavenly, I succumbed into unconsciousness."

"Well then, you now know why my babies' thrive. They are very sensitive to love currents. I haven't been living this life for nothing. Just you wait and see, if the old lady doesn't know what she is talking about."

Facing Death

I'M AFRAID THAT NOT EVERY HEALTH SCARE WAS MET with triumph. I can still remember one little rosy-cheeked baby who developed a hot little face and labored breathing that suggested something more formidable than a cold. I suspected double pneumonia, which the doctor confirmed.

I sent for the boy's mother, but his grandmother came instead. I was slightly wobbly from the motion of the fast train and thought the grandmother might relieve me somewhat with the sick baby. Instead, she remained downstairs and enjoyed herself to the nth degree, eating heartily and keeping the family in peals of laughter, which would occasionally reach my ears. While hilarity was at its height downstairs, I was on the next floor, hanging over a hot bath with the baby submerged. Each time I took him out of the water, he had convulsions; soon as I put him back, he would relax and open his eyes.

To make a long story short, my baby finally drew his last breath, the grandmother never once having come upstairs to even make inquiry as to his condition. Before she left, I made arrangements for the funeral, and when all was said and done, I could feel only that "God knew best," and that the little fellow had gone "to a land that is fairer than day."

In one of my broods of fourteen, I experienced one of the most heart-wrenching cases in my years of service. I had taken in a baby whose mother had passed away only thirty minutes after giving birth. She was a wonderful little girl whom I called Virginia June. At three months, what looked like an oval-shaped water blister developed at the nape of her neck.

I had the doctor look at it. As a result, a vaccine was made and twice a week a needle nipped her in the bud, which reduced it somewhat. Each time I headed for his office, however, a very strong feeling would come over me, the interpretation of which told me I should be going in the opposite direction. I saw another doctor, who had an entirely different approach to treatment.

"Even if it should be Syphilis," he said, "it will not be necessary or compulsory for you to part with her. Look how long I have worked with this vile disease, yet I have never been contaminated. It can be dealt with intelligently; the nurse will call you this afternoon and give the report. Give her the doctor's telephone number."

Late in the afternoon I was called to the phone. Expecting the nurse to give me the report, I was surprised to have her tell me to hold the wire.

"Doctor wants to talk to you." I wondered what had happened, but was not held in suspense very long.

"I told you this morning the case could be handled with no danger, if you wanted to keep the baby, but it's a 'Four Plus' case. I have to impress upon you the danger of handling her. Put rubber gloves on this minute, get into your car, take her to the hospital, and leave her there, no matter what your sentiment may be. She has enough poison in that innocent looking water blister to contaminate every human being in The United States. No wonder her mother died when she was born."

And I had been kissing the daylights out of her! The entire first week of her life, I had taken her into my bed and let her snuggle up close to me.

Three weeks later, the hospital called to inform me that my little girl had died. I cannot describe the heartache I felt. But this was part of the journey that God had put me on. And I had to continue.

Perhaps stories of this nature will cause you to turn away. But to those endeavoring to reach truth, happiness, and peace — perhaps through a different method — do not stop. For some unknown reason to me, the Arch Enemy attempts to thwart anything good. But stick to the middle of the road, and God is liable to suddenly make some startling revelation to you that you have been striving for for years. With God ever before you — with no barrier in the shape of money to obliterate the view and a cross indelibly stamped in the mind, just watch how God takes care of and protects you.

The Little Welsh Woman

❦

ON MY JOURNEY, I CROSSED PATHS WITH A LITTLE Welsh woman who wound herself around my heart. She was not more than twenty-seven. Her husband had been killed in the war, and the only other relative she had was an uncle living in Chicago who had recently lost his wife, leaving five children for him to try to manage. God had given this little woman a darling baby boy to ease her aching heart.

She was so alone over there that she came to this country to be near her uncle, and her baby boy was born in Chicago. All the uncle could see was the impossibility of her keeping that baby. She would have to raise his children, which made it impossible to look after her own child. Hers was to be disposed of, and out or an entirely clear sky, I was asked to be the go-between. Watch how good God was to put rough sense and nerve in me to break the combination. I realized that taking that baby from her would have been worse than death.

The bell rang, and there they were: the doctor and the Welsh woman, who had travelled two days to reach Chicago. Something was about to take place that struck me as taking advantage of a mother with a baby only three weeks old. Why, the shock to her nervous system, together with the sorrow of losing her husband, was sufficient to prevent her from thinking clearly. Think of the ride in an old, noisy, rattle-trap elevated train, up and down those steps, with a baby in her arms that she worshipped, and which she told me was the image of its daddy and the only thing on earth she had. Think what her thoughts and her feelings were to realize she was making this trip to give up her right to raise her own child. You see I was pretty well prepared to see what was occurring, but they didn't know it; not yet.

"It's a wonderful child, isn't it?" the doctor said, as if trying to goad me into snatching it up. "Perfect specimen, eh?"

All the time, I was getting hotter and hotter. But I remained calm. My thoughts were turning over a mile a minute; how to do it, how to be polite. I hadn't really the consent of the mother; she seemed to be afraid of her uncle and she was so weak. The only thing she intimated to me was that she hoped she would die when her baby was gone.

All this time, the deal was supposed to go through. Looking at the poor woman before me, I asked to speak to her alone.

"Now listen to me," I said firmly. "Answer me honestly: do you want your baby or do you not?"

"Oh, yes, I want him. But my Uncle..." and away she went over the same old rigmarole.

"I am going to make it possible for you to keep your baby if you will promise me not to change your mind."

The woman nodded, somewhat dazed, and we returned to the living room.

"Do you think you are treating this woman fairly?" I asked the doctor. "Don't you think you are forcing her to part with her child because she is handicapped and her uncle insists upon it?

The man looked at me in befuddlement.

"What does a man know about a woman's terror at parting with her child? Why should he be allowed to make her unhappy all her life? Why, that woman may never marry again. Do you realize what you are doing to her; that you are forcing her to part with her God-given gift? How can you do it and think you are right? I wouldn't want to look at a baby and know I had broken some mother's heart. It would mean unhappiness and misery ever before me."

"Well, that is all right," the doctor said. "But she can't afford to buy clothes. Why, she is so weak she can't even nurse him, and she certainly can't buy food for him. Baby food is expensive, and the older he gets the more it is going to cost her. Absolutely out of the question!"

"Well, I don't agree with you."

"What do you suggest then?"

"Why can't someone be found, to take care of that baby for her until she is able to take him? A month or two from now, she is going to be stronger. What seems at present impossible is going to look easy to accomplish."

"That's alright to talk that way, but where is the person who will take any child, pay all of its expenses, and give it back to its own mother?"

"Why, I will. What do you think I do? Do you think I am paid for my work? It doesn't mean anything to me to take one more baby. Look at the dozens I have given back to their own mothers under different conditions. Why, my work is a memorial to my son; it's my monument to his memory. Do you think I would desecrate it by prostituting my mother's love? What on earth is the matter with you? Can't you understand there are some things money cannot buy?"

I was so sick inside, and they knew it, and evidently realized the truth of what I said, as there was no further argument. I told the little Welsh woman to leave her baby, forget her troubles, and get a good sleep. Before she made her exit, I reminded her that I did not want her baby for myself. I merely wanted to help a grieving woman.

Now, isn't that a nice little story? Do you believe me when I tell you that the Welsh woman phoned me every Saturday for over two years, thanking me for what I did for her?

"I want you to know that you are ever in my heart," she

would tell me. "I never look at little Jackie and don't realize how wonderful you were to me. You saved him for me when my own flesh and blood went back on me, and I love you for it."

Another wonderful experience occurred when I met a lone father who had courage and sufficient intelligence to demand his children back. See, his twins had been put in my care for reasons I was unaware of. I never expected to see the parents again, and so I found a fitting home for them. When I told this to the father, he became despondent.

"I married that girl because I will never have it said of me that I drove any woman to a life of shame. I didn't love her at the time, but later a love sprang up inside of me for her and our unborn babes. I happened to bump into her one day, and she casually advised me of her condition. I was surprised, to say the least. Alone that night, I thought it over, and the next day I forced her into a church and married her. And now, I want my babies."

In all my experience I have never heard a man talk like that. He was a revelation to me, and my heart went out to him. No longer afraid of him, I asked him to sit beside me in the swing.

"I'll trust you with my babies," he continued, "if you'll get them back and raise them for me. I'll pay their board; I'm making good money and will come to see them once a week!"

I knew there was no possibility of retracing steps that had already been taken for their adoption. But I didn't let him know. Instead, I bound myself to a promise that I would make it possible for him to see his babies within a week, without knowing if I would be able to carry it out. A week is pretty good breathing space, and with telephone communication I found the mother who was arranging the adoption. He reclaimed his babies, as well as his wife. Now, I call that a real hero — his Croix de Guerre should be emblazoned with diamonds.

Freeing My Brother

❧✦❧

IN MY YEARS OF SERVICE, BABIES WERE NOT THE ONLY ones I saved. I had a very sick brother, the closest friend in all the world to me. His nervous breakdown, due to overwork, I discussed with another brother. All I could gather was his terrible plight. I was intent on helping my poor brother, but I was met with skepticism.

"What do you think you are going to do?" my healthy brother asked me.

"I'm going to bring him home with me where I can watch over him."

"You are just as crazy as he is. Use your sense if you have any. They wouldn't even let you get on the train with him. Forget it."

For two days after, I had him constantly in mind. I hadn't seen him in years. I'm not sure he knew I had raised nearly a hundred babies, more or less, in the preceding four years, so naturally he didn't know I had a very definite belief in God.

Finally I arranged with my daughter to take care of my six babies. It's the only time I ever allowed a baby to be touched by anyone else, but it was for a good cause and surely she could manage for three days. Then, I called my doctor, with the hope of being accompanied by someone who could help with my adventure. He advised me that he could send an associate with me for a price of $150 per day. When I heard the figure, the first thing I thought of was how much I could do for my babies with that sum. I told the doctor that I would let him know the following morning.

That night, I went to my room early. I closed the door, placed a reading lamp beside me, and opened a little book on prayer. I read that chapter over many times, begging God to give me an understanding.

"Please help me," I prayed. "Show me how I can go alone. You know I can't afford to spend all that money; I need it for your children. Please give me courage to go alone."

I just begged for a better understanding, and the queerest change took place in my mind. The doctor got smaller and smaller in my mind, and I kept feeling stronger and stronger. I felt so light, and something seemed to take complete possession of me. By morning that Doctor's importance had faded.

"I have decided to go alone," I told him over the phone. "I am not a bit afraid, and I have sense enough to know whether

I can do anything or not. I will call up as soon as I get back with him."

I bathed all my babies, giving each one a little extra hug. One was a deformed little thing who had spinal trouble, and his hands had been clasped tight since birth. I called him "praying Jesus," — but not in a sacrilegious sense. His ears were all out of proportion to his body, and deformed looking. He looked almost inhuman, but he had improved when his little cheeks became fat and a wonderful color. While he had once been a disgrace to the family, he was now a subject of interest and pride. His Granddaddy, the last time he saw him, was so happy when the little fellow opened his hands for the first time in his life and was able to hold an apple in his fists.

"If I could keep one of you," I said to the little one, "you are the one that should be taken, because, little darling, you would be saved a lot of suffering, and I doubt whether anyone would be bothered to take care of you the way I do."

Those thoughts were in my mind, and thought is powerful.

On the train, I pulled out a bundle of yarn and began to knit. "Get thee behind me, Satan," I said to myself. "You are not going to waylay me now. You are too late. I am on my way to Victory, and I will return with my brother. God will help me."

I deboarded in Newark, New Jersey and took a taxi towards my brother's home. On the way, I stopped for supplies. From experience, I knew the way to reach any man is through his stomach, so I stopped at a restaurant; got two club sandwiches, individual rice pudding, and a pie. That was about all I could collect that wouldn't spill. Knowing that he was always fastidious and particular as to his personal appearance, I stopped at a drugstore and made the necessary purchases that would make him look respectable for our return trip,

When I finally arrived, my brother's wife was surprised to see me. Some people get so excited, but she was upset.

"Are you going to see him?"

"Yes. And I am going to take him back to Chicago with me."

"Well, I won't go with you."

"Don't worry; I don't want any outside influence or negative minds. I want to be alone with him."

"You are not welcome here," the woman said. "Do not meddle in things that are not your business."

"Your husband is my brother, and I just happen to understand him. Now don't let your jealousy or selfishness interfere with his freedom. His life is at stake, and I'm paying the bills, so there isn't one thing for you to worry about and I may as well inject right here, that through my baby work I have been given an understanding of God, and that combination is impossible to break also."

"Go to see him," she said dumbfounded. "He has asked for you and seems to think you are the only one able to help him."

And so I set out for the sanitarium, where he had been

relocated. I kept on, going upstairs and then down, then through narrow enclosures. Finally, I saw him. There he was, with legs drawn up in front of him and his hands clasped around them. He was looking ahead, just as I might sit and look at the ocean if I ever had time. When I saw him, my feelings turned over inside of me. I was almost overcome with grief, but I stopped myself.

"If I break down, where is the help coming from? He needs help — not sympathy. Action is the right direction."

With an unaffected "Hello, there," his eager arms were soon around me. He hugged and kissed me and addressed his pals in misery.

"Look boys; here she is. I want you to meet my sister. I told you, she would come. She is the only member of the family who understands me. Isn't it refreshing to look at her?"

My dear brother then turned to me and got down to business.

"Did you come to take me out? I can't sit here any longer; I want to get busy." He followed that with many expletives, which caused the guard to shrug.

"You see how he curses..."

"You should really hear my ability in that department if I was placed in the same position. I dare say you would give me a medal."

I didn't sit there very long after that. My brother wanted me to walk off with him, but I explained I would go up to the office and talk to the doctor, and tell him the result. He became hopeless at once, accusing me of doing what everyone else had done before — namely, leaving him with promises to return.

"Now is your chance to prove to me that you are willing to let me run you for the next couple of days. I am going to the office, and I will see you later."

I plodded up that long, winding hill, realizing I was asking too much to expect any result from this strange doctor, but I kept going. I finally reached the office and met him. I told him my mission and asked if he would consider letting me take care of him. He listened to me and was very pleasant, but stated flatly that it was an absolute impossibility. Not getting discouraged, however, I insisted I understood my brother better than anyone else. What he needed was love, and he would get the best care from me.

"He'd smash everything you own."

"Well, I'm tired of everything I have and they have furniture sales every six minutes in Chicago. I'll take a chance."

"Alright," the doctor said. "I will let you. But you can't take him alone. You'll have to have an attendant."

And I agreed. Anything to get him home with me.

I went back to my brother and told him I was coming the next day. He was really angry that I would not take him then, thinking I was bluffing and would not return.

"I'll be back in the morning," I assured him. "Be ready."

I then called a one-time schoolboy acquaintance, who was

now an influential New York businessman, for help in transporting my brother.

"I'm going to take J. home tomorrow and I wondered if you'd drive here to the house and get me and then we'll pick him up. I don't think there will be room in a taxi."

"My God Almighty! Woman, are you crazy? Why, he'll kill you. I went to see him last week and I was glad to get out alive."

"Don't worry; the law requires me to take an attendant. I will sit with my brother, and you will be protected."

The next day we called at the sanitorium. My brother was in a nervous condition, throwing kisses to people on the street, but he wasn't acting half as crazy as supposedly sane people do on New Year's Eve. He wouldn't touch a drop of liquor no matter what he was celebrating, and I know supposedly respectable women who get drunk as fools, so I just looked at it from his angle and kept going.

By this time we had reached the station, and when the train came, my brother balked because he discovered the attendant was going with us.

"Alright," I said. "I'm going to get on and leave you to decide for yourself. If you are discovered alone, you'll go back, and I'll never come near you again."

He followed me. I told the attendant to get in another car and not let lay eyes on us until we landed in Chicago.

Once we left the station, I began to console J.

"Skrootch down Sammy. I'm going to carry you back to

our childhood days, when you and your little Muzzer used to worship each other and the rest of us were jealous because you were the pet."

When I mentioned "little Muzzer," his pet name for our mother, he relaxed and lay back, and I talked one incessant stream of days gone by. Every once in a while he'd shudder, and then refer to how dreadful it was in the sanitorium.

"Now get my system," I said. "Don't look back one second, not one thought even; turn your attention to the present and absolutely detach yourself from everything that is unpleasant. That's the way I get along in my baby work. I have done it so many times it has become second nature. You are able to press the button on or off, and think what you please, when you please, and you'll see why I have such a marvelous time all by myself. I work from morning to night like a troup horse, and I don't let anything else bother me."

We arrived in Chicago on time. Everything was perfectly normal until he saw the attendant, whereupon he became antagonistic and refused to ride in the same machine.

"Remember what I told you on the train. Forget other people and what they think, as that can't affect you. You make your own heaven or hell, and you will only give them just grounds for thinking something is the matter with you. Come on, let's go." And off we went.

My brother was treated as any one of the family. He never had a treatment or a doctor near him; just loving, kind, humanitarian acts. I allowed him the same privileges when it came to eating, as I did my starved babies. Either he was being held where he should not have been, or God made that rescue possible.

One could not possibly realize the wonderful thrills that I have had when God made it possible for me to look at someone in distress and treat him as I would wish to be treated. He made me understand that to be forgiven, one must first be able to forgive. Too much book learning can cloud this morsel of truth. Some people are so full of "knowledge" that it becomes necessary to use a sledge hammer to loosen them a bit. Don't think I am not thankful for six years of common schooling. But to live this life, it has been shown me that five minutes of Latin is sufficient, as "I love" is all that is necessary. My sure-enough lack of a higher education prevented me from becoming conceited and taught me subservience to God. Let the man or woman who would judge me first put in an apprenticeship of twelve years in the same spirit in which I have. Then that person will do his shouting in an entirely different key.

A Bout with the Police

ONE DAY, THERE WAS A TERRIFIC RINGING OF THE doorbell, that did not require psychic sense to interpret. I hurried as fast as I could, only to find a man with eight babies — eight of them! — waiting on my stoop. What else could I do but give them the love they deserve. I did not accept a cent from the man, who promised he would be back when he could.

Not long after that, good old Dave pounced into the room.

"You're in for it now, alright. They are going to arrest you. The patrol is out there waiting for you."

I thought he was kidding me, trying to scare me but one glance out of my heaven, but then I saw a great, black wagon at the curb. While I knew I was innocent of any wrongdoing, the thought of three policemen struck terror within me. I thought of how I might get around them, thinking back to the tactic that works with men as well as babies. First, catch their eye. Then, make inroads through tempting and satisfying food. Last but not least, appeal to the heart.

I went to the door, with a dear little bald head in each of my arms. As I started my downward flight, that same wonderful something took complete possession of me so that by the time I had reached the landing, I did not care if I had to face the entire police force.

"What is the matter? Please make it snappy because I am busy. These babies and six more have to be fed."

Without invitation, these burly Irish cops spread themselves all over the reception hall, each one filling a dainty teakwood chair.

"We are in a hurry too. Your statement that you have eight babies confirms the complaint against you. You are running a baby farm, and we have been sent to get the particulars. We have heard that you are selling babies right and left, and that you are living off the proceeds."

I made no attempt at defending myself. Instead, I asked them to take a peek in the nursery. Now, here's the exact spot where The Reality of God in my life stood out in bold relief. While my attitude gave ground for more suspicion, I could not get angry or even indignant. Instead, I felt sorry for those so narrow-minded and offered renewed thanks for my privileged life.

We were now on consecrated ground of the nursery. I

stood at the head of Virginia June's bed. She had been lying on her little tummy, half asleep. At the sign of us, she stood up and rubbed her head on my hands. Then she tossed it back and held up a tiny mouth to be kissed.

"You tell these men where you were when I found you," I told her. "Tell them how you tore all of your bed clothes into ribbons. Tell them how darling you have been ever since your visit to this house, and just because your new mother believed what Jesus said."

I moved along to the next bed where the angelic smile of Kenneth greeted me, the one whom I had named for my willing sacrifice, my dear Kenzie. Beside him, I came upon an empty bed.

"This was where Lotus slept," I told the policemen. "She was a darling, but had a cleft palate so I gave her back to her mother as I was moving to California. She's dead now; her mother also. They think she jumped in the lake. That's where you would find the mothers of these other babies if I hadn't taken them into my heart."

One would think that a trio of policemen would be able to keep rock-hard expressions, but I had touched the humanity in them. They were no longer authorities, but human beings.

"If one of you men had a daughter who birthed a baby out of wedlock, where would you rather have the baby — in my home with me for their mother, or in a foundling society? If one of you accidentally was the father of one of these babies, where would you rather have your baby be? Suppose you were absolutely destitute and this home suddenly came into your life — would you go to one of the various organizations where they treat babies like numbers? Now, let's bring it right home. Supposing that you men were these babies, where would you rather be? Here with me, or in an institution?"

There was a sustained period of silence before the leader of the trio spoke.

"This is an eye-opener to me. I am going to tell you something. Do you know when you were standing on the stairway, the sunlight was falling through the big bay window, and it landed on your white hair? I looked at you with a baby in each arm, and I felt all creepy inside. I never wanted to cry so much in my life. I don't know just why I should think of Jesus, but I did. I do not know what else to say."

"Thank you," I said, with a warm heart. "I do this only for God's love."

"If any of us ever get in trouble, we will know where to come," the man said with a merry twinkle in his eyes. "And the Lord only knows, I hope it will be soon."

So ended my near approach to a patrol ride.

That was not the only time that the police came into my home. Once, an officer was sent from the Humane Society on behalf of a complaint that I was beating babies! I met the man on the veranda and immediately felt that he was not ferocious.

"Excuse me for not looking up to snuff. I've been up all night with one of my babies. Poor little thing — she has a rash that makes her scratch herself raw. Once she gets started, the rest of the babies follow suit. So, to put a quick stop to what could be pandemonium, I clap my hands as hard and loud as I know how. They stop like magic!"

Immediately, the man understood what a neighbor had mistaken for the sound of the babies being slapped. With suspicion assuaged, the two of us spent a very pleasant hour together. As soon as his Ford was raced into high, a neighbor came in.

"What did he want?"

I recounted the story, which seemed to confuse my new guest.

"Didn't you feel like putting him out?"

"Lord no. He was my friend before he left. He gave me a little pat on the back and told me I was courageous to stand the various forms of onslaught."

The Law and its Tightening Vise

THAT WAS NOT MY ONLY RUN-IN WITH THE AUTHORITIES. Returning one afternoon from an outing with some of my babies in the nursery baby carriage, the Pierce, the butler greeted me with what seemed to be a handful of literature. From his manner and "I told you so" expression, one would rightly guess that he had perused the contents.

At dinner, with a little self-satisfied chuckle, he took this opportune time; with the dessert he "served" me these papers. To think that I was getting crucified for living with brotherly love — and this, the Enlightened Age! They included a litany of objections to my work — for no good purpose, of course — demanding compliance to rules that had no logic or reason. For instance, I was to receive permission from each neighbor living within fifty feet of us to be allowed to have these motherless, unwanted babies in my home. After experiencing the wonderful thrill of spontaneous combustion that opened my home, my arms, and my heart to helpless humanity, can anyone imagine how ridiculous it seemed to get neighbors' permission to carry on my work? According to my Spiritual experiences and interpretation, I was simply following as God directed me.

Why consider man in the question of serving others? My time was my own. If I chose to spend it serving God, by saving lives, whose business was it? If I chose to spend my money that way, instead of going around the world picking up curios, whose business was it? Acquaintances who had globe-trotted often remarked that my nursery was the most wonderful sight they had seen since leaving God's country. For Twelve Years it kept me intensely interested and occu-pied, but the authorities could not understand this. They had heard of those who either contributed their money, or their time, but had never met a surrender of everything material. And something else that interested those sufficiently intelli-gent to take cognizance thereof was where I got my energy. The answer, which they could not understand, was my Vision of Jesus. You'd be surprised to know how hard it is to smash ideals after staying on one path so long — even if those ideals do not make sense. I suppose that's the moral of the axiom learned in my school days: "Habit is a cable; we weave a thread of it each day, until it becomes so strong we cannot break it."

To cut to the chase, I had no choice but to hire an attorney. He did a wonderful job of communicating with clarity and reason, as captured in his letter below, but unfortunately it fell upon deaf ears.

Chicago, March 5, 1919

My dear Judge,

I epitomize as briefly as possible the following data regarding Mrs. Louise Sullivan, who lives at 826 Kenesaw Terrace, in accordance with our conversation of Tuesday afternoon in your Chambers. Mr. Sullivan is very wealthy and owns a beautiful home at this address. His wife was a widow before her marriage to him, and some years ago lost by death her oldest son. As a wonderful and beautiful memorial, Mrs. Sullivan began some four years ago her work of caring for and rearing babies with most loving and intelligent care until they developed sufficiently, physically and mentally, to be adopted into homes of the very highest class, by the statutory proceedings. I have handled some of these proceedings myself and know how careful Mrs. Sullivan is to see that her wards are placed only in the best of homes. I have always personally and most carefully looked the people up in addition to make sure her judgment was right.

In four years she has thus mothered, for greater or lesser periods, over a hundred unfortunates, and I regard her and her work, and my own little part in it, as one of the real bright spots in life. She now has ten children in her home, who are in this sense permanent guests.

A few weeks ago the City Health Department began serving notices upon Mrs. Sullivan to take out a license. After reading the ordinance, knowing her as I do, I concluded and advised her that in my opinion it would not be feasible or best for her to try to work under a license. She is naturally independent, being used to having her own way, which 99 times out of a hundred, as far as her babies are concerned, is the best way, and I know she would go straight up in the air on the first occasion when some City Hall Inspector or volunteer reformer, who did not know a thousandth part as much as Mrs. S. does on the subject, would try to dictate to her what to do.

Each adoption proceeding has always been as much of a wrench at her heartstrings as if the child were her very own, because she is very much attached to "her babies" and to part with six of them at once is going to be of considerable strain to her, but she has nevertheless concluded, much as she regrets it, that the best thing to do is to turn over to the proper authorities six of the little ones which she has in excess of the three which the ordinance permits her to keep without a license, and as soon as this can be accomplished, she will take the remaining lucky ones with her and her husband to Florida for the balance of the winter, as is her custom. One mother is claiming her own child.

I accordingly submit the following data, which is all she has regarding the six children constituting her "surplus stock."

- *No. 1. Boy; about 22 months old, parents married. Parents have at intervals, both before and since the birth of the child, separated and lived apart, and then together again for various periods of time; when he was about four months old, Mrs. S. discovered him in a nursery, and his pathetic little look made such an appeal to her that she did not rest until he had joined her family. Both parents appeared to be irresponsible and worthless, and whether living together or apart, spend most of their money and much of their time sitting around in cafes. Though friends in the Police Department have personally tried in every way to locate both of them but without success so far. This child is beautiful and as bright a youngster as you, or I, or anyone else, properly situated, would be glad to take into our home.*

- *No. 2. Virginia; about 14 months old; father and mother married; father is insane and in an asylum; the mother is normal mentally; is industrious, has a position but has three other children, of whom all are mentally abnormal and in some institution. Little Virginia was also mentally unbalanced, given to fits of temper, with apparently some* premonitory symptoms of epilepsy, or the like, and was very difficult to handle. She tore her clothes and bedding to pieces, and was absolutely unmanageable. It became clear that they would turn her over to some public institution unless Mrs. S. would take the child, which she thereupon did in her usual big-hearted way. Never for one instant after Mrs. S. took her did she in the slightest degree show any signs of her former mental condition, no temper, no ill health of any kind. While Mrs. S. does not like to think of parting with her, she is thus forced so to do.

- No. 3. "Brown Betty"; about 6 months old; parents are married; Mrs. S. took the baby when it was two weeks old, at the mother's request; the father went into the army; the mother stated she was going to live with relatives until his return from service, and promised that both of them would come and take their child. The father is now out of service, the mother has stopped corresponding; letters and telegrams have been returned and apparently they have left for parts unknown.

I will cooperate in every way possible, and so will Mrs. Sullivan in seeing that the best possible arrangement is made for the care of these little ones through your Court.

Your investigator will not find in Mrs. Sullivan the cold

blooded, high-brow, ultra-scientific type of university-bred sociologist, but rather an intensely maternal, red-blooded, snappy, high-class lady, chock full of good, common sense, knowing everything seemingly that it is possible for one woman to know as to the care of both sick and well children, and with plenty of means at her command to attend to them.

Under the circumstances, and in view of the City's unwillingness longer to permit her to do this work, I trust, with your cooperation, she may be speedily relieved of her charges, and beg to remain.

Yours very respectfully,

C. E. S.

This legal kerfuffle unhappily resulted in all but three of my babies being taken away from me. You can imagine my sorrow when I had to submit to such a cruel end. I had worked like a Trojan over these babies, until at last I had received a bit of silent encouragement that means a wonderful thrill to any mother. And then, with little notice, a group of licensed welfare workers who were duly "carrying out their order" took them, without so much as asking what they were being fed. That night, after feeding my remaining babies and making them comfortable, I gave a sickening glance at the empty beds.

Of course I stayed informed on the status of my babies.

Upon phoning, I learned that one of them was very ill. In less than five days, she lay at death's door after being taken out of my care. I felt compelled to announce to the world: "That baby has NOT been treated properly, or it could not be in its present plight." But God did not choose me for that kind of work. Instead, I remained calm and followed His direction to where my baby lay huddled in a room where there was scarcely space to walk. There was my little darling, unconscious. She had been exposed to a very infectious disease — Erysipelas. She died the following day. My dear little Polly, denied her birthright: a mother's love.

I am not a reformer, but an individual who has lived according to her interpretation of life. I worked under God so long and with such good results, that it did not seem right to offer the protection of a man-made license that ultimately means nothing. Babies should be protected by the Hand of God; no one without spiritual understanding should be allowed to come in contact with anything so sensitive and impressionable. Perhaps I am describing the ideal. Well, that is the only way to get the best results with a baby. I have proven it. As long as this world bows down to man-made laws and allows itself to be hampered by them, this world will be crippled.

Forget the narrow mindedness that a license flourishes under. In its place, plant a real desire to serve for a higher purpose. Throw off your fetters! You will then be able to see the good I have endeavored to do. So long as man allows himself to be hampered by confining and limited man-made laws, just so long will this world be retarded, and babies at least will be made the innocent victims. That is what this world has to come to eventually. What babies need and are entitled to is Mother love, not keepers.

Babies, more than anything else on earth, need protection, and the very ingredient that makes a baby thrive is spiritual understanding and maternal instinct. The order to get a license was the very barrier that prevented welfare workers from seeing what I was accomplishing. Can you imagine a law that incentivizes a woman to care for a baby with the promise of money? I did not care to be classed with such a class of people. In infancy the twig is bent, and what the baby needs is unlimited mother-love given freely with no monetary consideration. The work is in the interest of the child — not because you need twenty dollars a month to buy shoes and stockings for your other children.

Have service to God in your mind in place of money when it comes to the care of a baby. Then see how soon the expression of any baby changes. And that is why my babies all looked alike. Whether the mother happened to be twenty years old or fifty years young, there was a definite picture of the Christ Child in my mind — and that same expression was stamped on those babies.

Kenzie as a Young Boy

Kenzie as a Teenager

McKenzie Lowndes Memorial Nursery

Mrs. D. F. Sullivan
826 Kenesaw Terrace
Chicago

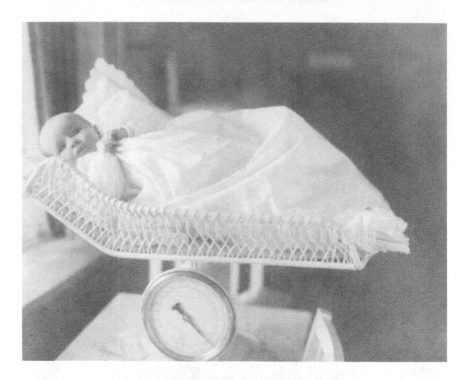

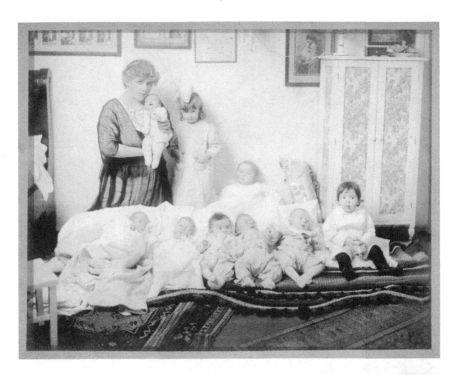

A Doubting Doctor

WITH ONLY THREE BABIES ON MY HANDS, I GOT THE bright idea of filling up a couple of afternoons with dancing lessons, while the babies were napping. For four years I had been going like a steam engine. I had always heard that a man who had been active all of his life and retires, either dies suddenly or loses his mind. I didn't care about doing either, so I found other ways of keeping occupied.

The dancing master was so English and so proper, and I liked nothing better than to shock him. One day right in the middle of the floor while we were twisted together in one of those intricate tangoes, our hearts palpitating, me trying to keep time with that syncopated rhythm, I told him what awaited me at home.

"I have the most darling twin babies. Only weigh four

pounds apiece; my, but I'm happy." With that dreamy music still going on, he broke his record and stopped stock still.

"My word, but you look jolly healthy and strong. You must be exceptionally strong."

As if all mothers were expected to be frail and weak. It goes without saying that I was quick to end my lessons. With no distractions to consume me, all of the trouble with welfare workers stirred significant concern in me. What would I do if they took all of my babies away? What would my life's purpose be? It was suggested to me, by way of a young acquaintance, that I seek the advice of a prominent doctor in the community. He had apparently directed thousands of people on the right road to success.

That sounded interesting to me, and when I learned that he examined women also, I made an appointment. Being advised that this doctor was somewhat cranky, I did my best to arrive on time. But with ten babies to feed, I got a little behind schedule. I grabbed a taxi and got there five minutes past my appointment. In I went, almost breathless.

"I'm sorry I was late; I had to take a taxi."

By this time I had removed my hat, because of course, you perhaps have surmised, I was going to have my head examined. But when I mentioned taxi, though, I thought the doctor would explode.

"Extravagance! Such extravagance! You shouldn't wear so many diamonds either."

Such was the start to our encounter. I wanted to ask him

what business he had whether I am extravagant or not, but I did no such thing. Instead, I uttered a truth that might get me into the man's good graces.

"I am sorry — I have ten babies to feed."

"Ten babies? What on earth are you doing with ten babies? Woman, you are wasting your time. You have the ability to meet the public and handle ten thousand, where you are doing the detail work for ten."

My head was whirling, and so was he. I felt about as big as a peanut — and not the Jumbo variety, either. Every time he uttered a ho-hum grunt that spells disgust, I felt as if I should have stayed home. I tried to explain my baby work to the man, but it was no use.

"Now let me impress on you, do not over-work. Strain either mentally or physically will finish you. Keep yourself under control."

You'd think I was some kind of powerful machine suddenly let loose, and I had lost the use of the brakes and was facing destruction.

"Another thing. You make yourself too common by mixing with inferior people," he said. "Hold your head up and get into the class where you belong."

And before me, I saw all the poor souls who had found their only happiness after they had come to my door. Inside, my heart sank and ached. All I could see was the steady stream of pink and blue blankets, bought for Fifty Cents, covering those wonderful bits of God's humanity in their mother's arms. Their offerings to me and my desire to relieve them of their load of trouble, even if only temporary. If I learned "big words" as this punk suggested, I would be cut off from all this wonderful happiness.

"Well, you can reserve that for someone else. My way suits me."

After that visit, I felt compelled to utter a prayer to God.

"Please, God, don't let me get so high brow that I feel above those poor souls. Don't let me get so I don't want to understand them. Please watch me; I'd rather bow down to them than have them afraid to come to me. You understand what I mean, God."

What that man expected me to be, I do not know. The worst thing is that in spite of the ludicrosity of his words, I believed part of what he said. After all, he was university-bred and I had no education to speak of. I didn't tell anyone of this encounter, save for my daughter Ruth. Only to her did I confide the doctor's discovery of my so-called "extravagance."

"You don't mean to tell me that you paid twenty-five dollars to find that out," she replied, laughingly. "I could have saved you that."

It is true that my mental faculties were questioned from time to time. I had psychiatrists and alienists state that I suffered from hallucinations, referring to my visions of Jesus. This, at least in my interpretation, proves that they did not understand the power of those visions. There was no doubting that I was an outsider — a freak of nature. Even a welfare worker could not help but to remark on my strangeness to one of my daughters.

"Your mother is a phenomenon. We all know that one is turned out every hundred years or so."

Reclaiming My Freedom

THERE CAME A TIME IN MY JOURNEY WHEN THE UNION between me and the man I once called "my better half" was severed. I did love that man for a time. To me, he was so necessary that I had a guilty feeling as though my love were idolatry. I even used to say to God, "Please show me how to live without him." I always got up at four o'clock in the morning to make his coffee, bringing it to the side of his bed and placing the dainty individual service on a tabouret beside him. Then, I would lie with my back to him to escape the smoke I so detested.

Do not get me started on what I did for him with his razors. He had a great need for them. In fact, there was only a certain kind that suited his particular kind of — well, I called it "a doormat"! The man had such beastly stubble that while he was away in Florida, I'd wire him: "Be sure to shave." Do not misunderstand me — he really was good-looking. But what men can do to themselves by letting nature have her own way is something terrible! To ensure that he would always have a sharp razor ready, I got a set: one for each day in the week, each duly marked Sunday, Monday, etc. That way, he could never make a mistake!

Now, I call that *service*. But do you know what that contrary Irishman did? He decided that it was less trouble to go to the barber. And so, his razors sat unused. I suppose it was too much trouble to remember the days, even though they were all plainly marked in gold letters.

After carrying out these acts of service — which were a pleasure to me, as is serving anyone we happen to love — in shoved the first wedge between man and myself. I was hood-winked, fooled and tricked by the same man within four hours. Thus, God opened my eyes to what was little short of idolatry. It is all right to be a slave to an invalid, but my service to a perfectly well man was ridiculous. Such devotion is intended for no one but God.

We are all in different stages of evolution. God does the joining, that is perfectly correct, but there is plenty of room for different opinions. Me and my husband were filled with them. I believe, very definitely, that God does not witness a marriage where contra-conception articles are neatly hidden in a suitcase. Using such materials disregards what marriage is intended for — namely, procreation — and thus, my husband put to rout the sacredness of marriage.

There was a continual struggle going on within me — between that love, and a deep adoration for Jesus. Ultimately, I asked to be relieved of my commitment to my earthly partner. It was necessary, I knew, for the great fulfillment of my purpose. In reminiscence of the wonderful life with my babies that I chose, filled with great satisfaction in the knowledge that I gained and the souls that blossomed from my work, I could hold no regret in the choice I made.

Divorce is strictly a personal matter, and those who think they are authorities on the subject and condemn it are wrong. Through experience both bitter and sweet, one learns that man is lover of the body and Jesus is the lover of the soul. It is possible, of course, for man to sniff at the soul. But not for long. It doesn't take long for him to get fed up with the soul and desire the body. Let alone the idea of ownership. Once I said my vows, it was as if I was now a subject who had lost her American citizenship. I belonged to him, body and soul, and was expected to do what he wished. My hair, for example. The idea of cutting it was sacrilegious to him! It took some time for me to summon the courage to speak my truth.

"You dare try to tell me that I can't do as I please with my own body? I want you to understand that my body is my own property, and that my soul belongs to God. No man can marry me and think that because he foots the bills, he can control me."

In two jiffies, I whacked off my curls. Not soon after, the marriage was severed as well. But you see, without doing so, my life would not have been possible. It was not until I severed the knots of matrimony until I had the chance for spiritual development. This life is the result of being a free thinking and acting human being with love as the motive power.

As soon as I heard the judge utter that the divorce was granted, I felt free and happy. Now, I could act upon the courage of my own conviction and face God in purity. I had lived so long in the lap of luxury. But for reasons best known to myself, I decided to smash every combination and get a million miles away. I wanted to be absolutely alone. There was a definite feeling inside of me to break every tie. I resolved to strike out with the babies on my own and move to California. The move was in the babies' interest, of course. I knew the climate and sunshine would be conducive to their growth, and I was going to continue my work.

When the divorce was granted me, I was the recipient of letters from the four corners of the earth. By then, the newspapers were filled with pictures of my babies and stories about my work, which elicited letters of praise and even offers of marriage. Think of it — just getting a bit of freedom, and here they were, with the halter staring me in the face. Some extolling my virtues to the point of calling me an angel, which proved how little they knew. They thought it a shame for me to live alone, where I was bound to become unhappy. This, of course, was an impossibility with the company of God and all the babies I had.

I must not overlook four earnest requests of men who wanted me to adopt them. Though their ages ranged from twenty-five years to thirty-four, they had not yet arrived at the adolescent period. One letter written by a Minneapolis man. In a very kind, gentlemanly manner, he enclosed a check for $50.00 to defray the expense of a drawing room on a train from Chicago to California. I got so sick inside when I saw the money.

"Never, God," I prayed. "I don't care what that phrenologist told me; I don't care where I land. Never will I touch a cent as payment for my service. This is my memorial; my hands and my heart, and I'd rather starve to death."

As considerately as I could, I mailed the check back to Minneapolis.

With a strong conviction and an enduring faith in God, I decided to buy a house in Pasadena, California without seeing it. My father had told me many times that I would be in my element in that little town, which was good enough reason for me to relocate. It certainly shocked my acquaintances in Chicago when I arrived at the Sheridan Trust Bank on a Saturday morning to dig up two thousand dollars, which I wired to Pasadena to close the deal. It wasn't until after the money had been transferred that I called my attorney to ask if I could afford the house.

Even my own family was puzzled why I had moved so quickly without consulting anyone. The truth, I told them, was that you have to work fast when the spirit moves you. I took no chances — I did not want to be influenced — and I went on my way.

So off I traveled to California with my baggage, my babies, and my parrot. Away from my husband and the big, beautiful home from which I had been virtually catapulted. For the first time, I realized women's importance in the running of affairs on this mundane sphere of ours. We are beginning to see that the hand that rocks the cradle rules the world.

A New Home, A Constant Duty

AT THIS POINT IN THE SPAN OF MY WORK, THE newspaper laws in the advertising section changed. No longer could unborn babies be advertised. This had the effect of saving me from buying a paper and reading the Personals. It also caused my name to circulate among people "in the market" for a little one. Everything and everybody came my way.

"There's a woman living in Pasadena, who will help you, if anyone can," people would say. The good old wagon did not break down when they came in with their loads.

The house was so crowded that I slept out on the porch. Each morning, I would awaken to another day filled with joyous possibilities. No one could understand that I chose this life by preference. I would choose to live on such a modest budget over indulging in the most exquisitely appointed banquet.

Why did I consider these babies my responsibility? Well, I believe that we are all part of one big family. We all readily repeat "Our Father" at church, but I ask you — what about "His children?" If it is a simple matter for Atlas to carry the world on his shoulders, why should it become a Herculean task for one lone woman to cater to the needs of God's helpless little ones? I never flinched at any stage of the life that was conferred upon me. And the reason I did not flinch is that I came into this world equipped to live a life that is an eternal struggle for happiness.

Soon thereafter, a fine looking man who introduced himself as a doctor called, expressing a desire for a tete-a-tete, with me. Now, who wouldn't live this life? I never knew who or what was coming next. The unexpected thrills! This being the enlightened age and realizing my especial privilege, I am going to lift the lid slightly by letting you see with Pandora's eyes. After being assured of my identity — a mother of unwanted babies — the doctor's first question proved there is always something to be learned.

"Do you take unborn babies?" He did not know that I had been offered seven within a span of four weeks.

"I'm beginning to think that is my specialty."

He proceeded to tell me about a case of two parents, both university graduates, who had become wildly incompatible. Though there was about to be a baby, they desired absolute severance of the knot via the divorce court, before it arrived out of fear it might bind them.

Feeling that a baby is what makes a marriage sacred, I suggested having the mother change her mode of procedure until after the birth. But I discovered that was out of the question. I then explained that my work was nearing its close and that I personally couldn't take her baby as I didn't work under a license. I would, however, be glad to talk to this prospective mother and possibly help in some way. So the Doctor left with that understanding.

The very next day, a couple called requesting a brand new baby. I gleefully related the call with the doctor, and as you could imagine they felt that they had hit a goldmine. I invited them over to discuss the matter further. The first thing they did was marvel at my little week-old baby.

"She's all I have," I told them, warding off any ideas before they took root. "I'm so used to having babies around that I'm lost without one."

Just then, the bell rang. Sitting in an advantageous position where I could see through the window, I told my guests what I suspected.

"I think that's the prospective mother now."

Excusing myself, I answered the door and confirmed my surmises. I invited the pregnant woman into another part of the house. It didn't take long for me to get all the details. While she talked, I wondered how on earth a prospective mother with her apparent intelligence, artistic hands, long tapering fingers, and well-shaped nails could cold-bloodedly dispose of her own flesh and blood.

"This is a peculiar situation," I told her. "There is a couple in the living room whom I take to be very refined people. They just came a few moments ago, and they want a brand new baby. If you are willing to meet each other, I'll introduce you and you can decide for yourselves."

And so, I led the grand march to the living room and introduced them. Any personal feeling that I might have had in not being able to mother the baby myself vanished with an inward laugh at the parallels between the two couples. Not only did they share similar names, they were both from Minnesota. In their conversation, it developed that they were acquainted with some of the same people and they had lived in the same places. Strangers one hour before, they left my home arm-in-arm, the prospective foster father very carefully helping the mother-to-be down the steps and into their machine, all of which I noticed and approved.

I was glad to be a link in the chain that could make such a timely and perfect connection with wonderful results. The baby was born three weeks after this meeting. He was legally adopted by the wanting family. Had I not known the circumstances and seen the mother before the baby came, it would have been almost impossible for me to believe that the adopting man was not the real father. He and the child were mirror images of one another.

Two years after this occurrence, I was put "upon the

carpet" and told flatly that I could not do what I have just related to you. Not even by word of mouth could I hint of a home for a baby. I have been the means of putting happiness into lives and relieving the tension of those in trouble. Through selfless love, and no monetary consideration, habits have been formed that were made by Divine Guidance, living and doing as God taught me. I leave it to you to decide — should I be considered guilty or innocent?

This was not the only time that doctors came to me for my services. One day, while I was in the kitchen preparing the midday meal, two Pasadena doctors arrived. Their hesitant attitude told me they craved encouragement to unload their grief.

"Come on," I said. "What's on your mind?"

"You have so much to do, we don't want to burden you."

"What is it, a baby?"

"Yes, and it's almost dead, and the parents are married."

"What's the matter; why don't you take it to the hospital?"

"The baby's so near death, it has one chance in a million, and we feel that one chance is here. If it recovers at all, it will be sick for five or six weeks. It's unconscious, with a temperature of 104.5. The mother knows the baby is slipping, and we are desperate."

"Have you spoken to them about me?"

"Yes, and they are willing to bring the baby here".

"Well, I'll try to help you, but be sure they understand that I don't want to be blamed if anything happens."

They went up to Prospect Place. While they were gone, I sent Douglas uptown for oiled silk and Antiflogistine because the baby had double pneumonia. I brought one of my little baby beds from the cellar, put it in a room where it would be alone, opened the windows, turned on the hot water in the tub, threw in a bath towel, took the unconscious baby's clothes off, wrapped it in another towel, stuck it in the water, and left it there until it was as red as a boiled lobster — watching it all the time, of course.

While this was going on, the Antiflogistine was warming; I laid a strip of oiled silk on the table, thickly covering it. Then I laid the baby on that, making sure that it wasn't too hot. I covered the baby's chest, folded over the silk, and wrapped it in blankets within its little bed. The strange part of this entire proceeding was that I was just left with that baby to carry out my own method of operation. The understanding was that the baby would stay with me for twenty-four hours, not coming back unless I called them. Now, that was a big responsibility, but I had God on my side.

At 12:00 o'clock midnight, I awoke suddenly and went downstairs. The baby was still unconscious. I warmed its bottle, but it made no attempt to nurse it. Quick as scat, I went to the kitchen, got out the double boiler, and put on Quick Quaker Oats. Then, I gave the little one a spoonful. It disappeared. Put some more in its mouth; it disappeared; and so on, until quite a good deal was gone. It was, in fact, a great big meal for a baby. I felt better and went back to bed without the slightest feeling of fear. When I came downstairs at 4:00 A.M., my usual rising hour, the baby was sleeping peacefully. It did not feel as warm as it had earlier.

At 8:00 o'clock, it opened its eyes and I got a hunch it might like some more Quick Quaker Oats. So, I propped him up again and the dear baby boy smacked his little lips and gave me a wan little understanding smile, as much as to say, "You sure know how to help a little guy."

My first thought was to call the parents. I was so thrilled, but excitement might start something else so I contained myself. At 2:00 o'clock that afternoon, one of the doctors called to see how we were progressing. While we were talking, the baby began coughing. It expelled so much mucus, it became necessary to hold the baby by its feet. After that struggle, which meant a good cleanout of all germs, the deck was clear for recovery, and the baby seemed bright. I sent for the parents, and they were thrilled beyond words. The baby had smiled; the first smile they had ever seen, and he was eight months old! On the eighth day they took him home. He had gained three pounds, and he went back as a spoon-fed baby. I gave the Mother samples of the different food I had been feeding him, so she could continue. I had the hardest time to convince her that I was not an M.D. This could not have been done under a license. In all probability, it would have ended with a burial permit.

My Feeding Formula

I SUPPOSE I WILL TAKE THE LIBERTY OF RECOUNTING THE "magic formula" that was responsible for the renewed health of so many babies. Pour the milk into a deep enameled pan. Then, add the Dextri Maltose and stir until thoroughly dissolved. Next, place the large sized strainer (with fine mesh) over the pan of milk, to which you have previously added the Dextri maltose, and rub the "Quick Quaker Oats" through it. Stir until all is thoroughly mixed; pour into large bottles and place in the refrigerator, warming only sufficient for each feeding (don't pour left-over feedings back into the main supply station). Babies show intelligence from birth and consequently know a good thing when they taste it. Unlike 'jazz hounds,' they do not like music with their meals, either.

My babies gain from one to four ounces each day with this food. In fact, one pair of twins put on one quarter of a pound for two steady months. Not once have any of my babies suffered from colic or constipation. When using this formula, be sure to make holes in the nipple larger than for ordinary food, as the mixture is quite thick and satisfying. Many babies cry at feeding time just because the mother does not realize the holes in the nipple are too small. At the same time, don't take scissors and make a slit — there's a happy medium.

Once, my formula was shown to a doctor who dedicated his career to the nutrition of newborns.

"Whoever made this mixture," he remarked, "just happened to hit the perfect fat content."

How could I have failed, with God as my coach?

If you are unconvinced of my formula's efficacy, I will tell you a story of a baby whose life was saved by it. He belonged to a dear little mother. I will never forget looking back at her as our car pulled away. Her steps were measured and her head was bowed, reflecting the sorrow of the compulsory parting of the ways.

And after looking the baby over, I decided to give him the first syllable of my own boy's name — Ken — because he reminded me of the cherished boy who had been snatched from me so suddenly. For as beautiful as he was, he proved to have a feeding problem. After three days of 'whooping it up' with such force that the food would splash quite some distance from the point of intake, I decided to visit a baby specialist. I would not tolerate the little one falling under his birth weight, and the extra job of cleaning up for him took far too much time, given that I was also looking after other children.

The doctor explained that there was an obstruction in the poor thing's throat, but that he was not well enough for surgery. I had no choice but to take him home and continue on with my special formula. Five times in the regular routine of the day, I'd feed him two tablespoons of what I called his "cement foundation." And what do you know, the little one learned how to keep it down.

Many times since then, I have taken bottle fed babies who were having all kinds of trouble. All of them have come to love my special formula. In fact, many doctors have been unintentionally cheated out of visits by passing on the result of my experience.

Religiosity

FOR YEARS I HAVE WONDERED WHERE MY STREAK OF religion came from, for it certainly skipped one generation. It is certainly not orthodox. A woman came to my house one day and asked me what my religion was.

"I don't know what you would call it. As far as I am concerned, it's "home brew." I try to help my brothers and sisters and preserve my decided love for God. That fact keeps me going pretty straight.

The poor old girl bristled up like a wet hen. She handed me a bunch of tracts and told me that unless I was washed in the Blood of the Lamb, my service to humanity was nothing and I was lost. I gave her a reassuring smile as she emphasized that last bitter statement. And, hearing a faint call in the distance from one of my last "shipments," I bid her a fond farewell. Of course, I did not accept the tracts. I explained that I did not have time to read them, and that she should take them to a place where they might be appreciated. She cleared her skirts of anything so unfit.

The basic Principle of my belief is that one Father presides over all of us, His children, exactly as though we were one big family. The broadening effect that this has had upon me, coupled with the wonderful power of my Spiritual Radio, makes it easy for me to ask others to join me, as if around a fireplace. With everyone comfortably seated, the next step is to picture this grandmother sacrificing her identity for the role of a self-appointed servant of God. I can only hope that everyone listening will endeavor to the best of his or her ability to grasp my meaning.

Let me elaborate by way of example. Upon request, I once attended the christening services of a friend's baby. This was during the Christmas holiday season, so every person paused at the entrance of the church to glance at the Christ Child depicted in the Manger. Inwardly, I thanked God for the unwanted babes that had been sent to my door over the years. I thought how wonderful to have attained spiritual development through actual experience instead of via the book route. After having various experiences, what chance would anyone have keeping me in tow with their thoughts? Could they demand me to believe their interpretations of the Bible?

I will now tell you about a very kindly elderly gentleman named Mr. Prichard who lived in our neighborhood. Each time a baby came to my door, he followed very closely upon its heels, always wanting to see what it looked like. Then on Mother's Day, he would manage to slip me a bunch of his choicest roses, without the neighbors being any the wiser. One afternoon, he strung together the kindest words into a sentence.

"After the sermon this morning," he started, "I spent over an hour with the minister, telling him all about your work — what a service of love it is and how you have never refused, no matter what the condition. I told him how I thought you were the best mother I have ever known. The minister could not understand it. It was the queerest thing. It made me wonder if he has ever listened to his own sermons!"

The man hit the nail on the head. The pulpits are filled with theologians — not those who actually carry out the teachings of Jesus Christ. Going to church is nothing more than theology. True religion is recognizing the Fatherhood of God, to the extent that you practice The Brotherhood of Man. True religion is following The Golden Rule, which is what our Lord and Savior advocated.

It says quite a bit that throughout my long journey, God has never given me the time to attend church or search the scripture. He has, however, stacked babies upon me in an alarming fashion! It never fell to my lot to join the happy throng as they went to the call of the church bell. Instead, so many little babies and children were sent to my door to wash, dress, and feed — it was in serving these little ones that I worshipped. With the Vision of Jesus indelibly stamped into my consciousness, I was continually reminded that He was watching over me, and I was happy reading the secrets in my heart. Through that Service of Love, I have seen a closeup of the real, living Jesus of Nazareth.

In my ignorance, I once thought that churches belonged to God, and that those privileged to officiate in houses of worship were representatives, morally bound to carry out Christ's Teachings. My experience, however, revealed that there can be a gap between churches and God. Leaving salvation for someone else to attain is one of the mistakes that cripples humanity. Churches are not for perfect people, and Jesus is The Only One who can rightfully claim that distinction.

I have encountered quite a few pious passages that feel utterly contrary to my experience. For example, I have never understood the all-too-common phrase, "Fear ye the Lord." How could one have fear where there is love? Throughout the course of my life, I have sustained constant communication with God. At any point, I could tap into my Spiritual Radio, and God's powerful universal broadcasting station would register my wavelength.

Here's another one: "No chance for spiritual development in a divorced person; it's cheapening." When I first read that, I thanked the heavens I hadn't seen that phrase before I started my baby work. But upon reflection, I decided nothing could stop a strong will like mine. The idea! No hope for spiritual development! If we were not all sinners, we would not have to be forgiven. As far as I have been made to understand it, there is hope for the lowliest person. Salvation for everyone. Just be sorry for the mistakes you have made, but prove your sincerity not by talk but by action, as talk is cheap.

I say to all of my readers — if they are at odds with one another, put God above the church. More Christianity in your "churchianity" is what God wants. More love expressed along the highways and the byways. Do and give until it hurts! There are entirely too many looking out for "number one."

It is all about freedom of thought. And when you have experience, you have the tools for that freedom, without having to accept someone else's ideals. For instance, one cannot deny that the man in the pulpit believes in a regular payday. And so, his complicated state of affairs leaves an imprint on what he says to the people following him. It is much better, I think, to develop an individual interpretation of God based on actual experience. An interpretation that is confirmed through the ebbs and flows of one's life.

When studying Jesus, civilization has spent nearly two thousand years concentrating on His death. I, however, believe in changing our tactics. If we think of Jesus Christ as living and then attempt to make him happy by performing acts of kindness, we will go a long way towards emerging from the present wilderness. Why not think of God as a reality? Why always think and speak of Him as mythopoeic? He is within reach of everyone.

God wants you to tune into your Spiritual Radios and show the rest of the world how to be peaceful and happy. It is so easy. Love God — then prove it by helping your fellow man. There are as many opportunities as one cares to find in this wonderful world that is filled with as many wonderful people. If it doesn't seem that way, it is just that you have not found the right combination yet.

When a babe is born, if every mother started out with an earnest desire to gain further knowledge and enlightenment as to what their special gift meant, there would be no war. Each mother would fully understand that her child could be called for service; that God placed babes upon this earth to generate love, to promulgate peace and happiness, and to be a reminder of Him.

The Families I've Known

✦❧✦

WHEN ONE HAS HAD MONEY ALL OF ONE'S LIFE AND ARE consequently used to handling it, it is easy to detect those who have had it. They never display the ear-marks of the nouveau-riche or the "get-rich-quick Wallingfords." Never snooty. California is world famous for the biggest in fruits, and when it comes to nuts, it has Brazil backed off the boards. The intense heat of the sun seems to have a bad effect on the brain.

That said, there are exceptions. I refer to an English couple whom I paired with a child to love. When this family left the United States, there was a grand farewell party at the Santa Fe Station in Pasadena. I had immediately thought not to accept the invitation as I do not drink, but I did want to see the family before the train pulled out. The place was jammed with friends, and the nurse-maid was laden with farewell gifts and train letters. It was hard to get near the mother, but I watched and took my first opportunity.

"My heartfelt thanks, Louise," she said with arms around me in fond embrace. "Tonight you are 'Louise' to me."

Nothing more; nothing less. I understood. I slipped away from the crowd and wondered if she had understood how thankful I was the Saturday before Easter, when she had come around to the backyard where, as per usual, I was hanging up the children's clothes before the memorial of Resurrection Day. And along with her gift of candy rabbits and eggs, she had the wherewithal to buy Nancy and Minto clothes I could never afford. They were tickled pink to have a belated Christmas celebration. God always sends someone at the most needed hour.

I began to realize that time was fleeting. Soon there would be shouts of "All Aboard," so I tremulously edged my way to a group of men. Extending my hand, "I wanted to say goodbye to the father, Percy, before the crowd milled around the back platform." He overlooked my hand and put his arms around me before his gathering of friends.

"Louise, I'm going to kiss you. You have done more for me than all these people put together."

I noticed that there was not the slightest trace or liquor on his breath, else the kiss would have been spoiled. As it was, his statement rang true. This was the only person in twenty years of service that I was forced to charge as I was absolutely penniless, but I did not tell him so. As I have already stated, I did have ninety-two cents to my name.

In contra-distinction to the foregoing episode, listen in on this. An altogether hoity-toity personage ensnared me into the following phone conversation. I was looking after her child at the time, as she was incapable at the moment, and in a decidedly peremptory manner and commanding tone, she leveraged a command.

"I want baby pictures!"

"I had been thinking of making a little album of all of my babies and making a gift of it. I have so many in different ages and stages, and tiny bits of baby hair with a reddish glint! I've been trying to get control of myself to do it right. But it is so difficult to find the time to photograph them, with everything else I have to do for them."

"Oh, we can easily blot you out of the picture."

And so it was clear that this woman had no interest in truly understanding the growth of her child. She had no appreciation for me, and she did not want to learn the full story of her baby's childhood. For I was inseparable from that tale.

Speaking of pictures reminds me of a foster-mother who could not get her baby to smile or even look serene for their first photograph taken together. There was some mysterious quality in me that made babies succumb to my tactics, no matter what they were. This is very disconcerting to notice especially after an adoption has taken place. So, what did they do? Nothing, except to cut me out of the picture where the baby and I were having soul communion. I understand and accept that I could not forever mother all the babies I encountered. But that does not mean that I should be cut out of their lives and forgotten. Albeit temporary, I was a piece of their upbringing.

Later in my journey, I encountered a woman whose thoughts on motherhood represented the very antithesis of my philosophy. This was one of the 20th Century Birth Control Brand women, who wished to remain a perfect 36-years-old. She did not wish to be bothered by the monotonous time required by 'Dame Nature.' She had fully bought into the work of America's best recognized businessmen, who forgot the idea that beauty is but skin-deep.

This woman inquired into my work, which I answered authentically.

"How darling," she said. "I have two of my own children, and I'm going to adopt two more."

"That's quite a family for these days."

"I suppose so, if I paid any attention to them. But when I adopt a child, I just turn it over to the nurse and I never really know the family has increased. I'll admit I am vulgarly healthy and supremely selfish."

I was really beginning to feel I would be perfectly justi-fied in carrying a sawed-off shotgun concealed upon my person. With birth control, one does away with the necessity of cradles. The spiritual foundation removed from any nation is bound to become top-heavy and the inevitable result: Destruction and annihilation follow! Watch your step.

Beware those who only care only about appearances. I encountered quite a few of these individuals, all of whom would have been better suited having dolls than living babies. I remember running into one of them on the street, with my five darling children standing in front of her.

"Oh, aren't they just wonderful, especially that beautiful little girl. Such wonderful curls, isn't she adorable? Now, why can't you get a little girl like that for me?"

I smiled, all puffed up inside. "Do you remember the ugly little thing you looked at a year ago? Do you remember how you told me she was not just the 'type' you wanted?"

"Well, of course."

"This, Dearie, is the same baby."

And so I deliver a message for all who endeavor to look after children. Pick up the ugliest baby you can find with God in your mind, and you will soon see God in that baby.

A Visit to Chicago

I HAVE BEEN ASKED: "WHY DON'T YOU PUT UP YOUR FEET for a few years? Take a break, and then if you want to raise babies again, do it when you can't do anything else."

That's just another point. Who wants a worn-out servant? Would there be any special significance attached to what you did if you just did it because you could do nothing else? In my way of thinking, I gave back to God for His use during the best part of my life.

No, I would not take a hiatus from my baby work. I did, however, take a short holiday to visit my daughter in Chicago. At the time, I had no infants and just one little girl, and I found the right kind of mother to look after her while I was gone.

On the train, I encountered a woman tending to her three children while her baby suckled from its bottle. While the mother was in the restroom, the baby was disturbed by a number of flies that had gotten into the cabin. Out of instinct, I calmed the little one, and the mother was happy to see the baby asleep in my arms when she returned. She proceeded to explain the troubles she had faced with the little one, who had slanting eyebrows and almond shaped eyes. The baby had a habit of letting its tongue protrude between closed lips, which doesn't add an intelligent expression to anyone.

"I had a baby who did the same thing. Just give him a few pellets of thyroid — he will become normal."

I soon received a letter from the woman. Her doctor had advised her to do as I had told her, and the baby was improving in every way. Its tongue was no longer swollen or hanging out, and the mother was very proud of him. That was not all — I was contacted by a stranger who wanted to speak to me personally over the phone. It was none other than the sister of this woman, to tell me how marvelous they thought my work, and how beautiful the baby had grown.

What a little world after all! An acquaintance of the woman who phoned me was none other than an employee of the Elite Catering Company, who had adopted several of my babies. All of them were doing splendidly, and I was reminded of the virtues that come when one forgets one's holiday and accepts the opportunity to perform good work.

While in Chicago, I had the luxury of reconnecting with babies of my own blood. One of them was Midget, my five-year-old grandchild who was already growing into a regular little football player. He was always stooping down with his head hanging between his wide-spread legs, signalling "One, two, ten, thirteen." He would then yell something to his Dad and they all seemed to get a thrill and make a rush; over went everything that stood in the way, and a good laugh followed. When he sat with me in the play yard, he always asked me to tell him stories about the trees.

One evening while we were waiting in the grounds of the Ladies Home in Altadena, I quieted him by attracting his attention to the hundreds of birds that find shelter in those beautiful trees. I just pretend they are boys, going to bed, and that they must finally quiet down and go to sleep or else they can't go to the football game tomorrow! It most tickles him to death.

One day, while his mother was at a card party hob-nobbing with fashionable society, he came to me for a "tree story."

"Midget," I asked the boy, "what do you learn in Sunday School?"

"About God."

"Who is God?

"Why don't you know, Nanny?"

"Yes, I do, but I want you to tell me."

"Well, God is the man who makes people. Who do you think He is?"

"That's a good boy! Who told you that, your teacher?"

"No, I just know that myself; what do you think?"

"Now listen, Midget; this play yard is covered with — what is that dry, ugly looking stuff?"

"Why Nanny, that is devil grass. My Dad rakes that all out. Gee whiz, but it is a very hard job. It takes Dad two days sometimes."

"I want you to know that when Nanny sits here in the yard, which is just sixty feet of devil grass, with all of God's children running around, it's like Fairyland to her in the midst of God's handiwork."

"That's nice, Nanny."

"And something else. When you go through grammar school and then to high school and college — when you have so much junk in your head that you don't know how to think — look back to the day when you were five years old and you told Nanny that God makes people. Remember that if you ever get lost."

"I know that, Nanny. That's why Mamma goes to church when she is tired and worried. She feels better when she learns more about God."

"I want to tell you one more thing, Midget. If you are ever fortunate to have children of your own and you notice that they have a tendency toward religion, don't be foolish through narrow mindedness and try to change their ideas. Encourage them to do their own thinking and follow it with service to their fellowman. And whatever they do, let it be because it makes them happy to help someone else. Don't ever think of doing anything for just the amount of money it is going to bring you. Then, when you are old enough you will under-stand why your Nanny was always so happy. Now, I'm getting in over your head, so you run along and play; this is enough for today."

As I watched the child run off, I was reminded how God had shown me in my work that He sees no difference in color, race or creed. We are all His children.

The Love Within a Headstrong Child

PICKING UP THE PAPER ONE MORNING, I FOUND A THREE-year-old child whom the parents no longer wanted. I phoned and met the woman, who had no trepidation about parting with him.

"Are you sure you want to part with him forever?"

"Yes, I do, and I can leave him tonight. He's really in the way and I'd rather keep my other children."

Well, I balked at that. It was too sudden, but evidently not so with her. The following Wednesday was agreed upon as the evening to bring him to me if she still wished to part with him. I sat waiting, getting more excited each minute and watching the clock turn. Around 10:15, the door rang. The mother and I exchanged a few hurried words — she had to go to a movie — and thus a darling little boy was left in my possession!

He didn't like me, wouldn't have a thing to do with me. I managed finally to coax him onto my lap and interest him in the different coins in a child's bank. For a few moments I would have his attention, then he'd start calling out.

"I want my mother."

I tried to get him to get to bed, but he had no interest in sleep. In desperation, I told him I was going and he followed, childlike. I had gained one point at least; but when I got upstairs, he started to balk again.

"Alright; goodnight; I'm tired; I have all my other babies to take care of and I have to get up early, so I'm going to sleep."

"Please, can't I get in your bed?"

"Don't you want to get in your own nice little bed? It's right here in the room with me?"

"No; please let me sleep with you."

"Well, alright; I will tonight." And with that, he gave one leap, with all his clothes on.

"Wait a minute, until I undress you."

"No, I don't want my shoes off."

"No sir, young man; if you're going to sleep with me, you are certainly going to take off your shoes, do you understand that?"

Now, in my way of being firm with any child, when I really want them to understand that I am the boss, that's my way of addressing them. In this particular instance, I certainly got a good laugh.

"Well — you'd risk one eye at least!" the boy said.

"No, sir, young man; you're not going to get into my bed with shoes."

"Well, I'll take one off lady".

"No; indeed you won't; you are going to take off all your clothes, shoes and everything, and get into bed the right way, or else stay where you are."

"Kiss me?" In a sort of half question, half request, edging up to me. "I'll take off one shoe."

Can you imagine! Well, if there is one thing I can do, it's kiss a child. I obliged his request.

"Kiss me again; I'll take off the other."

Think of the slow process; I began to figure it would be around 2:00 A.M. before I'd get him legitimately installed in bed, so I managed to work fast and got off both shoes and little socks.

"Come on, now," I said. "Let's get to sleep."

"Are you going to sleep with me?"

"Yes, Darling. Now let's say our prayers."

With the light finally out, that little fellow crawled into my arms. He was so tired, so worn out and so restless. At three o'clock he awakened, wide awake, leaning toward me, and running his fingers through my hair.

"You're my Mother, aren't you?"

"Do you want me to be your Mother?"

"Yes, that lady wouldn't give me away if she was my Mother. She isn't my Mother...you are."

At four A.M., he awakened and I assured him I was not

going to leave — I was just going downstairs to get breakfast started. I finished my other work and found him waiting for me, wide awake and not crying. After giving him his breakfast, he finally announced he was "all full up" on the last gulp of milk.

When I was working over that unpoetic spot, the kitchen sink, he pulled at my skirts and continually pleaded.

"Don't give me away, will you? Love me always, won't you?"

I was in a quandary from the very beginning when I first laid eyes on him. I saw where I was making straight for another heartache. The mother would surely return in time, and I did not want to lie to the little one.

Over the weeks to follow, I gave that boy a full childhood. I equipped him with little baseball suits, ball and bat, a swing, a Kiddiekar, and an assurance of motherlove when he ran in the house to find me.

"Tell me you love me. I want to hear you say it. Tell me I'll always be your little boy. Tell me you are my Mother."

I felt so guilty. He was so persistent, so grown-up and so understanding for just three years, I didn't know which way to encourage him. That darling affectionate child thrived until he was just like a rock, and I was being turned inside out between heartaches and happiness.

At the end of ten weeks, the Mother phoned me. The strain was on me. He made me strong, but it left its marks because I am only human after all. We were in the kitchen when the bell rang announcing her arrival. I hadn't told him she was coming. I thought as soon as he saw her, he'd naturally forget that he wanted to stay with me. I would have been much happier if he had, there would have been a load lifted, but I couldn't get him to go out on the veranda where she was sitting.

"Go Darling; your Mother's out there; go like a good little boy and put your arms around her and give her a big kiss and tell her what a good holiday you have had, and that you're glad you're going back with her."

And the little rascal threw his arms around me and kissed me so hard I felt guilty. Here we were in front of her, with him clinging to me. I sat on the couch and he climbed up behind me, and he hugged me so tight that you'd think I had bribed him to make her feel badly. And there she was, white as a sheet, head thrown back and trembling, looking like death. Talk about the most embarrassing moment of my life!

"Perhaps you think I have tried to wean this darling child away from you," I started, "but I haven't. From the very first day, he has insisted that I was his mother. It isn't right because the longer he stays, the worse it will be for both of us."

"I'm just paralyzed; I can't talk. No, I know him too well. He is so old in his ideas and so set in his ways that nothing could bribe him. He wouldn't go near you if he didn't love you, and that's what makes me feel so terrible. I know him."

"All I can say to you is this: "That child craves mother-love. You have only yourself to blame, and evidently he has found what has been denied him, so I advise you to change your manner toward him."

After over an hour's coaxing, the woman decided to take him. All his belongings were in boxes, but when I went to get them I found that they were empty.

"Yes, I hid it all. I don't want to leave my Mother!"

For weeks after, a little pair of socks would fall out from among my things. Shoes stuck away out of sight — even his baseball suit, all hidden! A pain would dart through me, and as the weeks went by, I thought I could stand the strain no longer. So, I phoned to see how he was.

"I found a beauty in him that I hadn't seen before," his mother said.

"Has he spoken of me?"

"No. He has never even thought of you since he returned to our home.

I was thankful for that. Perhaps the little fellow's secret longings had been satisfied. If I did not have the understanding that I have, my work would have been impossible. I looked way over the head of man, and with that dagger-like happy pain, I knew my service to God had been accepted at its true value.

My Childhood Beau

How many of you know what it means to come to California and be desperately homesick? How many of you know what it means to willingly serve God by laying down your own life — but in the doing of it, there's a loneliness that nothing can dispel. And then, just at the opportune time, to hear a voice from out of your childhood, reminiscent of "That Old Sweet Heart of Mine."

"Hello, Lou; I'm at the Biltmore. I'll be over as fast as I can get there."

The voice was familiar as anyone I had heard in my days. It was my beau from childhood. My first love. I suppose they call it "puppy love" when it's been plastered on so thick that you still get a thrill some forty five years after — and this is what happened when I heard his voice again.

Now, I was a widow, with nothing on earth to prevent me

from falling into his arms. I wanted to! To talk over old times - to rehash school days. My, I can't imagine myself holding any man's hand or head as I did his after smoking his first cigar! And then to be told:

"You're cold; why don't you sit close to me?"

He'll never know how much I wanted to, or how thrilled I was when I heard him say that no man ever forgets his first Sweetheart. And putting action into his thought, his arms were around me, kissing me, and I for a second, felt like smashing the pedestal upon which my high idealism had kept me.

I showed him the twins, John and Alice, then Gloria and Minto, all sound asleep, peaceful and angelic looking. He raved over them. How could I have so much love for them and be so cold toward him? When at the door as I bade him goodbye, I gave him the answer.

"Now, I'll tell you why I seemed so cold. I'm deeply in love. In fact, I'm engaged."

"Really?" he responded with a very hurt look in his eyes. "Why didn't you tell me before? When are you going to be married? Who's the man?"

"That's my secret. Some day you may possibly know, but promise me not to come back."

"Do you mean it?"

"Yes."

And I went back to my babies; the heartache occasioned by the farewell suddenly turned into thrills as I kissed Gloria goodnight. The truth is that I was engaged to God. And having lived without a partner in full service to my children — having experienced what it meant to be a spiritual explorer — I could not devote myself to a man of flesh.

Twas not very many months after this that I learned that our farewell had been final. My childhood beau had passed on.

After experiencing this chance encounter, I was reminded of so many memories from my younger years. I thought of an autograph album from my childhood, which had an inscription spoiling one of the pages.

"Ye must be born again."

Back then, I thought how inconsiderate to have that ugly scrawl through the middle of a perfectly good page. How could anyone be born twice? About forty years after seeing this phrase, I happened to be driving with a young lady who had heaps of education. In front of us was a flivver and across the window:

"Ye must be born again."

Immediately, the inscription from my youth flashed plainly before me with the full meaning. I wished to know her interpretation of the phrase, as she was so well-read.

"I guess you could be born again when you learn a lot," she said.

"It is more than that, I think. It is when you have an intense desire; when the soul yearns to be absolutely spotless and you live for the Spirit instead of the flesh and you wish to remain that way. I know because I have experienced it."

"Nanny, how do you get that way?"

"Working with babies for twelve years."

Now, if this story were to place me before you as an object of perfection, it has been grossly mistold. I am purely human. Don't get the idea of any saint stuff about me. It is not that I have any divine nature; it is that I fulfill God's will through my actions. I was conscious of being enlightened as one is when playing a piano and presses on the loud pedal to achieve more volume. Or manipulating the dial of a radio to get clearer reception.

It was not always easy. I struggled for something — not wholly understanding what that something was. I had an inner urge that was seeking expression, and each spiritual experience baited the hook in anticipation of what I might discover next.

Man shuts out the light, and God does not enter wherein He is not wanted. What God wants is heart action and sympathetic understanding — not hard-boiled pencil and pad figuring. That is not faith in God, but reliance on the so-called almighty dollar, and anyone with an ounce of intelligence knows that one has to renounce his own life to gain another's.

Parting with My Twins

❧❀❧

ONCE, A MAN PULLED UP TO THE HOUSE WHILE I WAS hurrying to get the babies' clothes on the line. I was preparing to take them for an outing, and of course the laundry comes first. I noticed that the visitor had a beautiful car. He had quite a bit of money — in fact, he was a millionaire. And he was looking for a child. I could tell, however, that the man was destitute when it came to love. I could not bear to give one of my dear babies to him. Instead of dropping my work and breaking my neck to see the man, I merely remarked that I was busy.

"But I will pay you," he said, dumbfounded. "Any amount you like, so long as I have a child."

"I am going to keep the ones that I have, sir. Good day."

Gee, did I get a kick out of telling a millionaire where to head in.

Unbeknownst to me, there was more to the story. At the very time that the man pulled up to my door, his wife was lying desperately ill and weak, unable to have a child of her own. She had sent her husband out with shattered hopes and clear instructions.

"Don't come back without a baby."

Of course, I knew none of this. I put up various stumbling blocks, but he vaulted all of them in his resilience. Finally, to checkmate him, I endeavored to speak in his language of the so-called almighty dollar.

"I have been offered three thousand dollars for a child. I promptly rejected the visitor."

"Oh," he said, under his breath. "I'd be willing to give you four times that."

"That is not what I meant! There is no negotiation — I just mean to show how much I want them myself."

But still, the man would not leave. I let him take a peek at Gloria and Minto, and then we passed the crib on the verandah. Up shot little John's arms. With a persuasive smile, he looked at the man.

"Daddy?"

As though in answer to his questioning tone, little John was in the man's arms. John was not a single child, of course. He had a twin sister — little Alice — who also took to the man. I must admit, I was surprised.

Eventually, the man left the house, but he was obsessed with the idea of having the twins. I suppose he had encountered his first experience of being refused something. But thinking back to John's reaction to the man, I permitted him to return with his wife the next day.

They were all smiles when they turned into the drive, especially the man. He spied the babies, and I gave the visitors the once over from behind my curtains. Out on the veranda, I encouraged them to search elsewhere for a child. But they insisted that these babies had made a special appeal; they had a different expression. Well, my sympathy got the best of me.

"Why don't you take them home for a few days," I said. "On one condition. I do not want them raised by a nurse. If you want them so badly, you will parent the little ones yourself."

To this, they agreed whole-heartedly. He rushed into the house, and she filled her pockets with little socks, suits, and dresses. Soon, the ultra-fashionable car began to take on the earmarks of a moving van. Out to the car we went. Alice looked somewhat confused, but my little old John cried as though his heart would break, and I heard him as they turned the corner on California Street.

Their little room was so empty. I had a feeling that they would not keep the babies any longer than I said, which is "until she got tired." Of course, I do not mean "tired of them," but "tired of working with and for them." I figured a single day of caring for Alice and John would put the mother out of business.

Needless to say, I didn't sleep a wink, and I was tired out from heavy heartedness. When I phoned the next day, they said they were simply wonderful — they hadn't cried or anything. Well, I had shed enough tears for the three of us. But when I called over the next few days, I did not hear the voice of the parents.

"They are downtown," a maid said. "They have been gone all day."

"Where are my children?"

"They are upstairs. She has a nurse for them."

I nearly fainted. Think of a hireling touching my babies, the first time the service had been connected with money! I left word for her to call me, which she did. She has the sweetest voice over the phone; so reassuring, until I told her that I was sending for the babies. Then I thought she was going into hysterics. I felt sorry for her, but what could I do? I had voiced the terms before giving little Alice and John to them.

It was not an easy affair, taking them back. There were tears all around — from the woman to the nurse looking after the little ones. As I walked through the gate of the house with the twins in my possession, I heard a distinct voice.

"Give them to them."

There was no denying it was the voice of God. Days went by, and still it haunted me. Finally I discovered something had happened: the wonderful, supreme happiness that I had experienced was never to be just as it had been. Try as I could to get the same reaction, it was impossible. Every bit of joy was gone, even when I sat in front of them to feed the twins. That electric, agonizing sensation of half pain, half pleasure was no more. Instead of their darling faces, I saw the sad eyes of the man. I heard the agonizing cry of the woman and that echo, "Give them to them."

It was impossible to disregard what I had been Divinely told to do. No matter what I did, that continual echo: "Give them to them" overshadowed everything. I was standing in front of the babies' laundry basket when I had the final experience in this connection.

"Do you love these children more than you did your own child?" There was no denying that it was the same voice that had been echoing through me for days. The voice of God. "You gave him to me."

A pain darted through me. "Oh God, please don't hurt me so."

"Did you not give your child to me as a sacrifice? Do you not love Me more than your child?"

"Yes, God. Please do not remind me, but make Kenzie understand."

"Give them to them."

Even with all that going on, I still hesitated. But then God continued.

"If you had only five minutes to live, is there anything you would wish to change? What would make you sorry if your whole life lay before you?"

Instantaneously, I saw my work of love, my gift to God blemished with this instance of not doing as He would have me do.

"I'd be sorry, God, that I had not minded You. I want my baby record to be perfect; just a record of love and devotion to you. I am sorry, God. Alright, I will."

That night over the phone I told them they could have the children inside of three days. The die was cast. That Almighty Power had sufficient influence to make me release those darling little children. And though part of me felt torn apart, my heart got as light as a feather. Now, my thoughts centered on how I could make the twins and their new parents the happiest. Early the next morning, I phoned the happy couple.

"You haven't changed your mind?" the woman said nervously.

"No. I just wanted to tell you that if your husband will come over some time today, I will give you the necessary papers. I want you to be happy. Better bring your attorney, and I will sign it; then you will feel safe to make your preparations and get their little beds ready."

They did come over in the afternoon, and I gave them the necessary signature.

"I have one request," I said to the parents. "Could I keep them for just one more day? My daughter will be visiting, and I would like her to say goodbye to them."

This favor was granted to me The next day, my daughter

arrived with her two little girls and the babies were asleep. She had only seen them when they were ugly little things and they had grown so beautiful. So when they awakened, I made Ruth and her children wait in the living room until I dressed them, and then with a little blue-eyed girl on one side and a little brown-eyed boy on the other, I walked in to show off my treasures. They just raved.

"Oh, Mother, aren't they darling?"

I didn't say anything except to agree with them.

When the children went out in the yard to play, Alice and John just stared at my grandchildren. I can see them crouching on the couch as though they had suddenly been let loose with a couple of wild men from Borneo! And I called out to them.

"You're alright! They are just full of pep; you know they just came from Chicago."

I was glad to have my daughter with me, but I could not get my mind on anything until the babies were called for and taken to their new home. While I knew I was doing the right thing, naturally I had a heartache. I knew that they would never again call me 'Mother.' I knew our relations would never be the same.

It's one thing to have a loved one taken from you by the Hand of God through the process of 'so-called death.' It's an entirely different matter to deliberately tear out your heart by releasing children who were made mine. With my thoughts on the material world, I could not escape the pain of giving my babies to a pair of millionaires. To me it was just like a dream; I could hardly understand myself.

While I was sitting in the swing, waiting for the moment to arrive, a woman unknown to me hurried in with a little boy about five years old. She had made a mistake in placing her little one in a nursery, and she had an appointment in LA on which her son could not accompany her. I calmed her by explaining it was alright to leave him. I was going to be home all day, and while my work was not on the lines of a day nursery, she could let him stay. What was the difference, as I had so many more do the same thing?

She apologized, thinking it was terrible to impose upon me, but I laughed off her concerns.

"I don't care when you come back. I'll look after him — he will be alright."

This welcome intrusion broke the pall that was hanging over me. Looking up the street, I saw "Cinderella and Prince Charming" coming — not in a carriage drawn by eight little white mice turned into horses, but in a wonderfully groomed car. Prince Charming in a gray suit, looking like he had just stepped out of a bandbox; and his wife just as immaculate and stylish, looking beautiful in a sport costume of palest yellow. Strange to say, the babies were also in yellow — an attractive foursome.

As they came in, I felt like raising my voice to the heavens and yelling. But in living a life like this, one has to be able to swallow. The new Daddy-to-be picked up Alice and put her on the front seat of the car. Her new mother took a seat with my darling brown-eyed John on her lap. Soon, they turned on California Street and I went back to the veranda, their little voices to hear no more. But inwardly, I knew I had done what God had been telling me for six weeks. My light-hearted, sad feeling told me that I was alright and my personal will had been mastered.

After they had gone I was in the back room feeding Minto, with my little grandchild, Barbara, sitting on a footstool in front of me. She, noticing tears in my eyes, and looking up at me so inquiringly, she asked me a question.

"Nannie, when you love your babies so much, when you love John and Alice as you do, why do you give them away?"

I was so completely floored that I could not answer. That from a mere child! If any adult had nailed me down that way I don't know what I would have answered, but they never did so I don't have to worry.

"Well, Barbara, you wouldn't understand."

"Now Nannie, promise me this. Promise me you will never give Gloria or Minto away. And if you are going to give them away, give Minto to Suzanne because she loves him and give Gloria to me because I love her. We will feed them and keep them clean and be good to them."

What else could I do but promise?

The day the twins left happened to be Suzanne's birthday, my little Chicago grandchild, and we had a tea party. The boy visitor had a good time. Isobel, Ruth and I were sitting on the couch in the front yard when his mother came up hurriedly at six o'clock and ramming her hand into her bag she pulled out a crumpled up bill, and sticking it in my lap, I protested:

"I don't want anything."

"Oh, yes, take it; buy yourself some ice cream."

"Well, I'm counting my calories now; don't you think I'm fat enough?"

Both Ruth and Isobel, killing themselves laughing. The mother was on the street by this time. Three times she sent the little boy back with different toys he had in his hands, until finally I bid her to stop.

"They are his; we have had a birthday party; he drew those."

And my daughters took the crumpled bill. After undoing the creases, they held it up laughing.

"Well, that's not so bad, mother. At least that's an improvement on the way you do business. It cost over $2.00 to keep him with the toys we bought him, but here's a dollar."

So I washed and ironed the dollar for fear of becoming contaminated by those who had already handled it for monetary gain, and it still hangs pinned to one of my baby pictures in Minto's room as the sum total of my salary for twelve years of volunteer service. It really should be put on exhibition.

The next day, the papers were filled with the following headline about the adoption.

"TWINS, CHILDREN SUDDENLY PUT INTO PROMINENCE THROUGH WEALTHY PARENTS"

I was certainly reminded of the power of money, but I didn't feel hurt or have the slightest feeling of regret, which proves to me the Power of God. The new parents phoned me that the babies slept all the way over and they were alright — so beautifully trained. They could not believe that I had managed to part with the children.

"We could never do what you have done," the woman even remarked.

"Oh, yes you could," I thought. "You could do just as I have done if you worked under the same Power and had the same desire for spiritual development."

Nonetheless, I had to accept that the twins had a bright future ahead of them with loving parents — even though I would not be one of them.

Forging My Path

THE FIRST DAY OF NOVEMBER 1927, I AGREED TO A luncheon engagement. I mention it only as a material vehicle through which was obtained a Spiritual experience. I will admit it was a very flimsy affair, apparently with more undercurrent and strength to the things that were not mentioned than the subjects of conversation. Gone one hour only in the middle of a beautiful Southern California day, so happy and light-hearted that I really enjoyed it, except that I missed Gloria.

Of course, as usual I put her to bed for her afternoon nap, and she was left sitting on the veranda. The very fact that I would make a break from home and children would be sufficient grounds to elate my daughter, who had come to stay with them. The sun was dazzlingly bright. Everything was so ideal that I experienced an intoxicated feeling, as though I was treading on air. It was so wonderful to be thoroughly relaxed and to not have to think of boulevard stops. Like all light-headed women, I was getting an extra thrill over the fact that I did not have a "borrowed garter," nor "something blue," nor thoughts on a wedding trip, although my remark must have been misleading.

"Gee, I feel just like a bride."

Well, I never married any man because I loved him. I married to have children.

My companion for the moment was glad to see me break away from my supposed irksome duties of home life and give me a little change, which he suggested should be forthcoming at least once a week. While he thought my work wonderful, I had entirely too much stick-to-it ability to be really healthy. He had invited me dozens of times, and I imagine that his musings were motivated by my continual refusals up to the present date.

Now, I wasn't going to waste a great deal of precious time on that man or any other, so I asked God to help me sift his mind and show me his line of thought by placing the right words in my mouth.

"Do you know what would make me ideally happy?"

"Now tell me, just what can I do for you? What is it?"

"I'd love nothing better than to keep on working the rest of my life for other people's happiness, if someone else would pay the bills. That's the only thing that stops me. I do not care a whoop about myself. No one understands me, but I get a wonderful thrill in my interpretation, when I know how to make other people happy and save babies' lives."

What a woozy look my friend gave me. Regardless, I continued.

"Just to love humanity for humanity's sake. If you want to get a real thrill, try it. I'm not even hungry now, with a perfectly good meal in front of me. Do you want my chicken?"

All this time I was watching with what gusto the man devoured his food. At the mention of money that man's expression changed, and my throat in turn suddenly became paralyzed. I could not even swallow water.

"Why a license is a protection; try to look at it that way."

God had shown me in a hurry that I had made a mistake. The same food on my plate was enjoyed by myself later on my veranda, for I carried it home in a box to escape my so-called companion.

You have gathered, I am sure, how contrary I stand to man-made laws. Would you advise people to work under unreasonable mandates if it made them so narrow and so blinded that they couldn't see the benefit when it was thrown right at their door? Wouldn't you say, "Take away the blinders and see the good that is in people" and make way for the God-given benefit that babies especially need?

Only once in the twelve years of volunteer slavery did greed ever corrupt me. That "once" was when I was given a beautiful wrist watch in appreciation of a service rendered. I was as excited as a child with a new toy, although I had four other timepieces. Well, I had been told that the two little hearts engraved on the back were baby hearts, which gave me an extra thrill. But later it occurred to me that I had been paid. My word — I never touched that watch again! But still, the guilt ate away at me. My Covenant made secretly with God in 1915 would have to be adjusted.

"God," I prayed, "I will part with Gloria if necessary; I would rather face You alone knowing that someone else had her than to have one thought blemish my offering to you. I am sorry, God, that I rebelled. You understand. Please God, cleanse me of my iniquity through the waters of baptism. I do not wish water just sprinkled over me, but to be completely immersed, so that when I emerge, I will know that every thought has been washed away. I desire from this day forward to walk in the newness of life."

What was that wonderful sensation that filled me completely with such a thrill of joy and satisfaction, and a tingling through my entire being?

"Better far to have parted with your little child," God told me, "than to have looked into her eyes with an unclean heart."

What thankfulness filled my soul! Only one with like experience could appreciate the revelation that I was given.

Nevertheless, no material pleasure ever diverted me from my course of action. If I was stripped of every vestige of materialism, lying prostrate upon the ground beside the hem of my Maker's Garment, I would not change places — even if it meant gaining the combined wealth of this world.

With belief in life everlasting, one is made to know that accumulation of riches means nothing unless God is in the foreground. This world has been running along for quite a while with money taking first place. Try placing God where man and money have been. All I do is to connect myself with God, and my result is harmony.

The only thing that ever upset me was the way wealthy people attempted to "Lord" it over me; just as though their money meant something. It was plain to see they did not know what I had willingly given up to be able to do just what I was doing. I was sufficiently human to get complete satisfaction, feeling that God must have seen something worthwhile in me to let me carry on His work, when some people would pride themselves on not being able to make a cup of tea.

If I hadn't the absolute knowledge and understanding that I was in constant communion with God, I could never have lived through one year. People just walked rough-shod over me whenever they got a chance, but I happened to be one of the fortunate ones whom God has chosen to do His work. He put in me fearlessness and will power to forge ahead.

Another Epiphany: The Birth of a Book

❧

IN THE MORNING OF THE FOURTH WEEK IN NOVEMBER, 1927, I donned my best bib and tucker and left Minto and Gloria with my daughter. Starting out in the business world, you must be alert. It is important to put your best foot forward and look prosperous, even if it is not true. Even if you get kicked out of the front door — pick yourself up, shake the dust from off your clothes, and go into the place you just got kicked out of.

The interviews were exhausting to say the least. It took everything I had to keep my professional demeanor, and in some instances I lost it.

"Say," one of the businessmen said. "I've known you long enough to know you're honest. After watching you all these years, you have always been at the same thing: children and babies. Where are they now?"

"Down at my daughter's."

"You must miss them."

I pushed back the tears. For at the mention of the babies, I had an inward spasm and prayed to be allowed to die right there.

"So long as I am able and as long as I can afford, I will take every baby I can get."

And here I was face-to-face with a man trying to talk business. I just couldn't do it. Money, though necessary, was obnoxious to me. What's to become of me? Don't believe in suicide and yet I know I'm different. It's a terrible calamity to befall anyone, materially speaking.

After interviewing with five people, I had four invitations to chicken dinners. Instead of going home happy, I was completely prostrated.

I drove down to my daughter's. One honk of the horn and the door of her house flew open. Minto darted out like a wild colt, bubbling over with joy, and was followed by that darling little Gloria with her beautiful head of curls. It was as if I had just returned from the North Pole instead of being gone for a couple of hours.

"Success?" my daughter asked me.

"Everyone seems willing to help me. They all believe in me."

"Why shouldn't they?"

"Yes, but I felt so queer when all my life I have been

giving to the world. Whenever I think of selling something, my mind turns back to Kenzie and my babies."

I was at the end of my trail. The million things to be done around the house had always increased my spirits, but something had changed. I was so depressed. What was wrong with me? Why was I alone in my opposition to the material world? I was tired to death with my mental struggle, all uphill, except for the attitude I let myself assume. I took down each separate article of clothing from the clothesline and seemed to drop as much as I pulled off the line. I stooped to pick the articles up and dropped another off the other side. I was so tired, so weary. Finally, I got a most peculiar inward sensation, as though God had complete possession of me and I was talking to him.

"This is my end. I am happy to go now; I have reached my limit of endurance. I have tried facing man. You know my innermost feelings, and it cannot be done. I can't stand the strain any longer. Please take me. Maybe when I'm gone, people will better understand. And even if my own three children are affected by my going, it is all worthwhile. Four lives and Kenzie's — that's a small number in comparison to those who have been made happy. I beg of you to put an end to my sorrow. I want to die."

I came into the house and prepared the food for the babies. After feeding them, taking one and then the other on my lap, powdering their darling little bodies and getting on their nighties, I descended into a darker pit of sadness.

"Please never let these darling babies shed a tear," I said. "Please let me see them with smiles on their faces, with a look of understanding that I am with them. That is all I ask; I am happy to go."

After saying their prayers and the little final good-night kiss, Minto in bed first, then up to Gloria's room, I went downstairs. Nothing could take away that depression. No one from the outside world could have guessed what was going on inside me. All I had ever wanted was to add some love and care into the world, serving God's will, but I could not stop bumping up against materialism. I had at least in the neighborhood of $30,000 in mortgages that I couldn't get a nickel out of to save my soul. I never knew one thing about business.

"God, why was I put upon earth with such high ideals that it is impossible to cope with man? If I am not right, then why do I have feelings that are so strong, so unalterable? What have I done wrong? Where have I displeased?"

And in final desperation, I was almost ready to cry, "My God, my God, why hast Thou forsaken me?"

But he had not, for the little instantaneous answer.

"Speak with."

I felt, then, that there was something else for me to learn. Something else for me to do, and I was merely being tested. But still, I did not fully understand.

The day after starting out in the business world endeavoring to sell stock, I was standing over the washing machine as usual, listening to the chug chug. With my head leaning on my left arm and my thoughts whirring rapidly, I sent a message to God.

"You know, God, that I do not balk because I do not wish to work. You know I'm willing to do anything, to keep on until I drop dead. It just kills me to get down to a material existence where all one hears is dollars and cents. After living so long in the clouds with You and my wonderful babies, I'd rather die. One can't make people see Your way, and You know those in authority are attempting to stop me in doing Your work."

Simultaneously, a clear image formed in my imagination. It was a row of dominoes standing before me, just as I used to stack them when I was a child. The first one toppled over, hitting the next with a sort of metallic click until the entire row was flattened. It was perfectly clear to me, then and there. My life was nothing but a single domino, but when pressed in the right direction, it could send all the others into action.

Then another image flashed in my mind. There were two figures. The first had a head covered with grey ringlets, which automatically suggested a replica of myself. And beside it remained our Lord and Savior, Jesus Christ. It was the same figure — the loving Jesus of Nazareth, the King of Kings who appeared to me on that never-to-be-forgotten 12th day of July, 1915 after Kenzie left this Earth. And I discerned through His smile what he endeavored to spread. That because he lives, we shall live also. With this ecstatic scene before me, He spoke in a patient, entreating voice.

"Why do you deny Me - why are you ashamed of Me?"

"I don't understand. I am not ashamed of you. I believe in you."

"When you know all this, why are you ashamed to tell the people about Me?"

"God, I'm sorry; I didn't mean it that way. Yes, God, You have been wonderful to me and my babies, Your children. All right. I'll do the best I can for You. I'm sorry."

There I stood, stunned, with a fixed image of what was expected of me. In these spiritual experiences, I was made to see that time meant nothing in the eyes of God. A thousand years mowed down as quickly.

"I don't understand," I said. "Do you want me to turn to the material world, or do you want me to remain on the path I'm on? What do you want me to do?"

"Tell the story to the people."

I thought back to that day in 1915 and the promise I had made. What was it that I had promised? To do anything God would let me do. Now, I knew precisely what that was.

"Yes, God," I said aloud. "I will tell the story to the people. I will show that You do live and that there is no death. Just as faithfully as I have endeavored to care for all of my babies — Your representatives — I will endeavor to explain how you came into my life."

The Process of Writing

AFTER THIS SPIRITUAL EXPERIENCE, I REALIZED WHAT A moral coward I would be to keep the past twelve years to myself. It was clear what I must do: write a book!

If this moment of awakening wasn't enough, God provided another forceful message. Just after this experience — out of a clear sky — I was stricken at about four o'clock in the morning while cleaning the refrigerator. I felt myself about to go unconscious, I phoned a friend, who found me collapsed on the front porch.

The doctor, a personal friend as well, laid down the law.

"You have suffered a stroke. No more of this slavery — you're overworked. No more babies. I've tried to stop you before, and now this settles it."

She called a nurse and ordered me to remain in bed. And as I rested, it was clear. God was trying to show me to get busy and write my story. It was time to shift my goal from the labor of looking after children to the labor of the pen. That isn't to say that I would abandon Minto and Gloria. They still needed looking after, and I would continue my duties, albeit mildly.

But still, the idea of writing my story made me shiver. As I struggled to push forward, a woman arrived at my door in want of a little girl. Her intention, which she candidly imparted to me, was to find a little one who could wait on her in her old age! I made it clear that I would never give a child to anyone who had such designs. She grudgingly accepted my position, and our conversation shifted to the Visions I had seen. How His expression of sadness in 1915 made me want to do everything in my power to make Him happy; and how His expression of triumph made me want to pen my story.

"Why woman, that story doesn't belong to you. That story belongs to the world. You're hiding your light under a bushel. You're one of God's instruments."

"I realize that, but we are all to a greater or lesser degree."

"You have received instructions," she responded. "Be sure you do as you're told."

After she left, her words began to make further impressions. The thought struck me that God had sent her for the reason of motivating my new endeavor. The next time I saw a friend who was helping me at the time, I made a clear request.

"Buy some pencils and pads when you're uptown. I am going to write."

When this friend returned with two dozen pencils and half as many pads, I was daunted by the task before me.

"Don't discourage me so," I said. "I couldn't fill one if I started from my earliest childhood memory up to the present moment.

My first attempt at writing was a real joke. Needless to say, it didn't coincide with the mental impression made upon me. Perusing my first sentences, I became desperate and tore the paper into bits to frustrate any detection of my foolishness. I decided I would have to take my punishment for not carrying out my orders. But God's face haunted me. I loved him and wanted to serve Him further.

"Man had attempted to stop my baby work, but You made it possible," I told Him. "So You must think I am capable of delivering this message. I will look to You, God, to help me."

Soon, my thoughts ran as smoothly as the Florida bayous. God was good to me, and very patient. If He had supplied Lindbergh with aviation beacons during his journeys, they would have been as weak and flickering as tallow candles in comparison to the brilliant radiance that emanated from Him.

The nature of this task was entirely secretive. My babies could not help me in the writing, and my family had no interest in my work. Not one ounce of encouragement, not even from those who profess thorough belief in God. In fact, my children dissuaded me from my efforts.

"If you ever dare publish that book, it will be your passport into a lunatic asylum."

"As far as the asylum end of it is concerned, there's one thing you want to remember; I never went into one that I didn't release somebody."

Nevertheless, it was clear that I was on my own.

After hearing my pen scratch for hours at a time, and knowing I had devoted most of my nights for three long months, I coaxed myself into reading the first few pages of my work. It was clear, now, that God was with me as I scratched at the page for hours on end.

So, I took the treatment. I got up and proceeded with my daily labors as per usual, allowing no one to touch Gloria or Minto. I had three massages a week while the children had their afternoon nap. At night, I stayed up through the dark hours to write this story. To keep myself from distraction, I permanently disconnected the radio and discontinued the daily paper. My inner feeling was that I didn't want to have my thoughts distracted by anything so commonplace to conflict with the import of my message. It was time to share the story that had been buried under blankets in a dark part of my closet since 1928.

When I asked God to help me write, I had no idea what I was doing. But I experienced a most thrilling seven months' session of night school in inspirational writing, usually commencing at midnight and keeping up until morning. While my own personality was injected, some things were so foreign to me that I'd stop long enough to wonder just what was happening. In the midst of something serious, a childish mind seemingly would blurt out something foolish, as though to irritate me or make me laugh. Now, the strange thing was that I'd write just as these things came to me, much as though I were a machine. When I'd read my sentences the next morning, I'd get a thrilling shock. It was as though the words had not been written by me.

As I wrote one evening, I saw before me a beautiful tree, symmetrical as could only be fashioned by the Hand of God. It represented Twelve Years of devoted service to God and man; veritably a Tree of Life whose branches were evenly balanced. At the pinnacle of this marvel, the Star of Bethlehem was placed, whose glorious radiance shed light upon the pathway. These wondrous spiritual experiences occurred few and far between the chug-chug of the washing machine, the buzz-buzz of the ironer, the drone of the Kitchen Aid, and the whirring of the vacuum cleaner.

Many times I've been asked, "What's the name of your book?" and I didn't know what to answer. I thought about it for quite some time as I wrote throughout the darkest parts of the night, but nothing came to me. Then, while I was preparing supper for the family, it floated to me through the ether — as plain as you would read a primer.

"THE ROMANCE OF MY LIFE: THE JOURNEY OF MY SOUL."

The absolute satisfied feeling I had was sufficient.

"Now, that's off my mind," I said aloud. "Thank You, God."

Before declaring my life the result of hallucination, try putting my ideas into action. Undoubtedly, you will be surprised! What marvelous things God can do when man forgets to put the stopper in his bottle of selfishness and allows it all to evaporate. Whether I be sinner or saint, I have lived a life fit for the gods, and no matter what the future holds for me, the past cannot be taken away!

After being assured of one's goal it is easy to progress. All we must do is work for mankind, thus co-operating with God, then experience. Then, by overcoming selfishness with one grand sweep, let's all move on toward Utopia, for everything that I wrote was in favor of Love instead of Law and ended in defense of God. That defense is closely followed by world peace.

My Pasadena Bungalow

My daughter Ruth always feared that I would become bankrupt. I suppose her fear was worth something, as my accounts dwindled to nothing over the years. Many people told me that I did wrong in choosing to not look out for myself. But I would disagree. I would not trade places with the wealthy, with all their money, ill health, and unhappiness. I am happy, healthy, and able to work. And I am proud of what I have done on this Earth.

Anyways, with so little money, I sought seclusion in a little bungalow to continue my story. I had no connection with the outside world — not even a phone. To keep me in touch with God, I had Gloria, Minto, and the two little twin sisters — Elain and Ilean. The house was defective in every detail. There was an explosion every time the furnace was lighted, which reminded me of school days.

The first night, after giving Gloria and Minto their bath and letting them splash to their hearts, I heard a gentle tap at the bathroom window.

"Please don't let the water run out of the bath," a meek voice called out. "It floods our yard!"

"Well, what will I do with it?"

"Throw it out the window!"

So much for moving into a house in livable condition. One would think this may present a distraction, but I had faith in the idea that it was all part of the process of getting my story out on paper. Thus began the crusade to construct a cesspool for proper drainage.

Now, do not feel sorry for me because every setback I experienced was really a boost. A poor old man was hired for the job, whose mission on Earth seemed to be to climb inside of a bucket and drop into a hole. By the depth of it, one could have mistaken him for locating China.

While domiciled in this little bungalow and through the generosity of a benefactress, Gloria and Minto attended a private school on West California Street. A friend took them to school each morning, but I always called for them at noon.

Many times, I turned the back of my car into sleeping quarters by using uprights and a full-size mattress. When finished it was so comfortable that the babies could have slept there through an earthquake.

Back in my Chicago days, I used to ask God to watch over my babies while I went out to get a new one. And of course,

He always did. Now, maybe some of you think that God is only in one place and that the same method would not work now that I was in California. Strange as it may seem to some of you, He is the same in all places and at all times when you believe in His reality. Of course, I needed someone of human form to watch after the twins when I went to pick up Gloria and Minto from school. That ended up being Mr. Long, a grand carpenter who proved to be a master mechanic in any line. He was practically rebuilding the house. Before leaving the house, I'd go wherever Mr. Long would be pounding, splitting, hammering or cementing — there was not one thing that man could not do — and ask him to look after the little ones.

"I am leaving now to pick up Gloria and Minto," I would tell him. "I should be back before the twins awaken. No need to stop anything — bang as much as you like!"

You can imagine the look that the man gave me. He nearly died of fright! His abilities were quite broad, but caring for babies was not on his resume. One afternoon, while I was bathing the twins and he was busy at a nearby window, we had an illuminating conversation.

"Some neighbors visited my house last night," he started. "They were all chewing the rag, complaining about how hard they have to work and how weary it is to live such a monotonous existence. They talked about how tired they were and the nuisance of that their work has to be repeated all over again the next day. I could not help but butt in. 'Talk about work?' I asked them. 'You don't know what work is. If you want to know the first thing about it, come watch the woman I'm working for. She tackles everything, from soup to nuts. Nothing stumps her; she lugs mattresses, empties the garbage, cooks, washes, and scrubs. She emerges from the scrub bucket looking like a million dollars, and with the air of one who understands that work is a privilege.'"

Wise Mr. Long. At least there was one adult who understood me.

Once the remodeling of the bungalow had concluded, I set a grand meal to celebrate. I laid out China, silver, glassware, and linens — everything to make a supper special. Gloria and Minto were spotless — for once, at least — and the heavenly twins were sound asleep in the corner.

"Come dear Lord, our guest to be," Minto called out, that wild and untamed colt with such a shaggy mane. "I'm sorry," he said, turning to me. "I forgot the rest."

I assured him that that was quite alright, and we proceeded to eat.

"Mother," Gloria started, "why does the same food that we used to have in the other house taste better here, tonight?"

And so I was reminded of the wisdom of children again, even in my advanced years. They do not care about riches — only love. And this, we had in excess.

Little Fritzie

Your Depression apparently did not teach me anything. I say "your Depression" because it has never been mine. Anyways, saving was never a strength of mine — not for my own benefit, but for that of my babies. After my family would give me fifty cents for the necessaries of life...oh boy! I would give it away to the first person who walked down the pike, who looked like he needed it more than I did. With the coins gone, I would turn to face the Risen Son.

"Just as I am, Lord. Please take and keep me, just as I am."

Just then, the phone rang. I answered to find a friend on the other end. Years before, I had watched over her son, little Fritzie. She had then loaned me twenty dollars, which I was unable to pay back at the time. You can imagine my discomfort at hearing her voice.

"Hello, Louise. What are you doing today?"

"I'll be glad to see you if it is about the baby, but if you want money you might as well stay where you are as I haven't any. I expected to settle my account this month, but I just got a letter that the person I have been receiving forty dollars a month from is now stuck. I suppose everyone is feeling the Depression."

"Don't worry about that. I have something that I'd like to ask of you."

I wondered what it could be. Maybe she wanted me to help her sell vegetables — I sure got a laugh out of that. You know darn well that I would push her right into bankruptcy because I give everything away! And if a poor, hungry-looking mortal with a bunch of half-starved straggling children at her heels passed the stand, I would be liable to take the little one in and lose all profit.

"What is it?"

"Well, I was looking over the books this morning and decided to clean up everything that was possible. If you have anything that you would like to give me — a coat, a hat, a dress — anything will do as I am clean out of clothes and haven't the cash to buy a thing. Aren't conditions terrible? We can't collect a cent, and I need a coat so bad. It's so cold standing on the damp ground all day."

"I have lots of things that I could give you," I started, "but they are not practical and would never amount to as much as

I owe you. You could get a very good coat with prices as low as they are now, and I wouldn't want to take that advantage of you."

She still insisted, so I made a raid on my closet and dumped an armful of coats, dresses, and hats on the veranda. I loaded them into the car and delivered them to my friend wearing nothing but a sleeveless slip. I had little else to wear.

"You see what I mean," I said to my friend, showing her my wares. "None of this amounts to the actual value that I owe you."

But she had her own ideas. She spied a fur-trimmed, gray bongaline, late afternoon wrap. I had chosen it because there was a pinkish mauve tinge running through it that matched my hair. She put it on and went to a cheval glass. With a questioning smile that now made her otherwise plain fat face very attractive, she turned to me.

"Do you mind if I take this?"

"Sure, you can have it, but I still don't feel right about it. That doesn't square the bill in my mind."

"You don't owe me anything. Look what you did for little Fritzie. Your food put fat on his skinny legs and arms. He had a small frame, but you filled it out and made him sleep so that me and my man could rest at night. Believe you me, that's worth more than the twenty dollars right there. You don't think I could forget the day that you came over to my shack to feed him and put the mosquito netting on so the flies wouldn't eat him alive. Any doctor would have charged me ten dollars for a formula, at least, to say nothing of phone calls."

"I could never charge you a cent for helping Fritz."

"And I don't think you know what a thrill I get with this coat on! I'll wear it the next time Johnny and I go out in the evening — he sure will be proud of me when I wear something that belonged to a swell Pasadena lady."

In that moment, my mind went back to a stormy day, when I went driving with "all my little keedies." It had been pouring, the side curtains all up, with confusion and racket coming from the back seat. Everyone knows what children sound like when cooped up in a closed automobile. Everyone also knows the treachery of a mud road — built up high and with deep gullies on either side — and what a grand invitation awaits a heavy Pierce Arrow to "Slide Kelley Slide" until we gently sank up to the hubs. Stationed for life — unless the good natured citizens took pity on us, as they did. After four hours of strenuous labor — the handling of planks, the clinking and clanking of chains — the continual pushing back and forth of that heavy bus — I gave her some gas and off we went.

What kindness that afternoon! No one was thinking about material thoughts — just the helping of a neighbor in need. I can still see those men with mud up to their waists, working to free me from all that mud. That is just what I have done my entire life — help people who have been stuck in the mud. The only difference is that I have spent more than an afternoon doing the work. Not many in this world could understand that, but the mother of little Fritzie did.

The Neighbors Who Saved Me and the Neighbors Who Spurned Me

❧

I HAVE TOLD YOU THAT I DID NOT WORRY MUCH ABOUT the Depression, which puzzled people quite a bit. The spiritual foundation that I had developed made the Rock of Gibraltar look like a boat in the ocean, bobbing up and down, and no market crash could rattle me. With this wonderful foundation, everyone was suspicious of me. I was told to my face that I was not telling the truth; that I had money stuck away someplace. Well, I was prosperous — but not from the materialist's viewpoint. I had had many spiritual experiences, and I knew that I simply had to keep working until it killed me. Then, I would be able to occupy my home and achieve Prosperity in its mightiest form.

To the material minded — how did I manage when I had only fifty-two cents? That is just the point. In 1915, I placed my life in the Hands of God, and now, I cast my burdens on the Lord as He has told us to do. I had done my part by following Where He Led me, and I gave everything away — even the roof over my head. It was up to Him to see me through, and I knew He would. With this foundation, one is never tempted to take a shortcut to the other side of the veil. It is both instructive and interesting to "stand by" and watch how God gets one out of a hole. I'll tell you how He did it in my case.

God uses His people. He sent the right kind to me. Baker, farmer, grocer, dairyman. My bills piled up, sky high, but these wonderful souls helped me. For the most part, white-collared church-goers raved over my work and supported my labor. These providers continued to supply me with daily needs, free of charge. *Why?* Well, because God put a definite understanding in their hearts. I will provide a specific example in my butcher. On one boiling hot afternoon in Pasadena, a very self-possessed, pleasantly smiling man entered the living room at my invitation. He was neatly attired in a grey suit and tie with a blue edged handkerchief peeping out of his upper left pocket. I almost envied the hanky — to be that close to something so wholesome and clean in thought, action, and deed.

The last time we met, he was behind the counter with a cleaver in hand and a white cap and apron on, looking to give me the best in poultry, steaks or chops. There were three brothers and two sisters; all worked together in their market. Always smiling, always pleasant—eager and willing to take a dozen extra steps. During the Depression, their system of operating changed to try to meet the different conditions. Their treatment of me was the only thing that never changed. Always the best they had, with usually four of them hauling things to fill up the back of the car. Then, when the door was slammed and the little ones were chewing on their cookies they sent me off.

"You sure you haven't forgotten anything?"

"No, I think this will hold us for a week. Not much chance of starving with such service. You'll all be wearing diamonds, yet. Just don't lose hope."

"How about your book? How is it coming along?"

"Slow, but sure. I do not see any sense in hurrying. I feel it is worth my best effort. I don't want to publish it and then afterwards think of a million things I should have said."

"There is a lot underneath the surface. You will never be deserted after doing GOD'S WORK!"

This from my butchers who barely knew me! Their kindness went on for years, ending with me owing them close to five hundred dollars. And still they were friendly! After an intervening year, the head of this firm was now in my living room, nonchalantly twirling a straw hat while waiting for me to be seated.

"You look prosperous," I told him, "even if you did have to

shut up shop. I was sorry to hear about it. My daughter told me how deserted the corner of Huntington and Fremont looks now. I am more than sore to know that I can't pay you; at least not at present."

"That's tough luck for you to be left stranded after the way you have taken care of everyone. But that's humanity for you. Just pigs. Don't think of anyone but themselves. I saw plenty of it. I know you haven't anything. I'm not referring to you. After the life you have lived for those babies and children and seeing the women that come in the store smoking cigarettes and wearing pants, why, I'd prefer to give free food to you over them — no matter how much cash they have. Well, there'll come a time some day when they find out a thing or two."

Why would a man have that attitude toward one who owed him such a sum? Because he was decent, I tell you. Because he understood that there are more things in life than money. Of course the butcher is an exception to most. This is the problem with the world — hogs are running it.

H - O - G - S — in capital letters. You have men who go to church every Sunday with sermons passing in one ear and out the other, and then demand to have their bill settled while the rest of the world suffers. And then you have the butcher, who never had the time to go to church but practiced what Our Lord advocated: the Golden Rule. Give me the butcher every time, and when you all follow in his footsteps we will have World Peace.

The material individual, however, is not entirely to blame. It is partly the fault of the masses who, through their ignorance, place upon pedestals money as something to worship. They do not honor those who lay down their lives for the betterment of humanity, and they do not give a tinker's whistle for upright character even though it is necessary for democracy. Character, you see, is not something that can be erased by time. Character is a lifetime in the making — not something acquired overnight.

Now, while God sent help to me through some men, there were other men who were calling on me to help themselves. Men, who prior to the deplorable condition of the world, had filled high positions but were now forced into mediocre work — that is, bill collecting. My only regret was that I had not spent more money, or more correctly speaking, that I did not owe more money. Think of all the extra acquaintances I would have made.

To avoid those men, I always talked in big numbers and made flat statements. When they discovered I had saved all these babies' lives out of love, they became immediately interested in my welfare — forgetting entirely what they had come for. Consequently, we spent many pleasant afternoons discussing the merits of my book. And I did not find one single dissenter. Instead, I felt the glad hand-clasp of well-wishers who had come for money or the promise of it. They left me with encouragement to plod along because their mission had led them to one woman who knew God and relied upon Him implicitly. I will never be able to tell how close I felt to all of my brothers. Having been removed from the flotsam and jetsam of struggling humanity, it was a joy to discover that I could still connect with people who did not make caregiving their primary concern.

Fending Off Amnesia

DRIVING FROM MY HOME ONE BEAUTIFUL MORNING with three children in the back seat, I was intending to visit a sick friend, my one-time chore-woman, who was now in a convalescent home. As I was about to turn a busy corner, I was attracted by the nervous actions of a bareheaded woman. Instead of making a turn, I stopped. She instinctively came to me, putting her hands up to her eyes and peering into the car window. Just a momentary flash of nervousness overtook me; the children were somewhat startled to see a strange face so close.

One did not have to be a Sherlock Holmes to know that she was lost. There were people all around us, and as she drew her hand across her forehead, as though she were trying to unearth her thinking apparatus, there flashed before me what I needed to do. Though this person wasn't a baby, she was one of God's children. She required help, and that was what she would get.

"Listen to me," I told her. "I realize your trouble; you've forgotten who you are, haven't you? Come on and get into the car with me. I will be your friend."

She looked at me with the expression a child has, whom you attempt to lead and wonders why you are interested, but never doubts your kindly attitude. I helped her into the car and closed the door. I didn't know who she was or how she would act, but I had faith that God would help me. I was helping a poor soul in distress.

"What are you going to do with me?"

"I am going to take you to your home. This is a beautiful day, and I have three darling children. Turn around and look at them."

As she did, Minto, only three, who seemed to sense conditions, asked me a question.

"Lady sick, Mother?"

"No, she is just tired and we are going to drive her home."

Thinking to reassure her by my positive statement, I addressed her.

"I want you to feel perfectly safe, so I will stay with you as long as is necessary. It is a wonderful day to drive, and I will just go slowly along until you remember who you are and where you live."

She answered, "I don't know and I can't think."

"Well, you are just scared now, and that is naturally

clouding your memory, but there isn't a thing for you to worry about. I am perfectly happy trying to help you as I haven't another thing on my mind."

And why didn't I have? While I sat with that lost woman, the same wonderful thrill was filling me; the same confidence that I have always had when handling my babies. I did not feel as though I were with a stranger. I had the feeling of the whole world being akin. I was doing the most natural thing, trying to help her find herself, just as though she were my mother.

I soon learned that the woman had spent all of her money, and although she had a bank account, she did not know what name to sign on a check, even if she could locate it! We had been driving about an hour — in and out, up and down — drawing her attention to the beautiful flowers. Finally, crossing a railroad track, she lit up.

"If you turn this way, I think I can recognize the street."

She begged to be let out of the car, then, saying that her family would be suspicious if they saw her get out of my strange machine. And so, the woman was returned to her home. To show you how the material, normal mind looked at it when I related what had happened, my daughter said:

"I don't see how you had enough nerve to tell her she didn't know who she was."

It never struck me as being "nerve." I was just doing what was put in me to do, and besides, she felt that love flowing from me to her.

Minto's Name

IN THIS CHAPTER OF MY LIFE, MY DAYS WERE ALWAYS
difficult. I never progressed easily — it was always two steps
forward, then forty steps back. But bit by bit, I moved along
my God-protected path. Never was I off my feet — not even
when I suffered a great wound to my foot at three o'clock in
the morning. Since I was always tending to my babies while
they were awake, the wee hours of the night were my only
time to tend to the house. I was mopping the babies' bathroom when the mop handle flopped onto a glass, which in
turn struck the stationary stand and embedded a shard into
my instep.

I was not immediately conscious of the deep cut until I
stooped to pick up the pieces and discovered I was in a pool of
blood. The way it was spouting out of me reminded me of

water mains being flushed out on the street — only this was bright red coming from me. I looked around for a towel to make a tourniquet and found nothing except a bath towel. The slightest pressure on that foot — spurt, spurt! And my other foot was slipping in the gory mess.

I managed to get to the couch and elevate my foot for a few hours before Minto and Gloria woke up. I knew in the morning that I had to push through the injury, as these two little ones relied on me. No one else had ever fed them before. And so I continued my work, neglecting the fact that I had severed an artery.

One day, Minto came running to me, crying.

"Now, what is the matter?" I asked.

"Why didn't you give me a decent name?" he asked me. "Everybody makes fun of me."

"What do you say back to them?" I asked the poor boy.

"That my mother gave it to me. And then they say that that old white hoot owl is not my mother at all!"

And so I knew that it was time to tell Minto about the origins of his name. See, in the final days of my father's life, he was losing strength rapidly. He knew that his time was coming to a close, and he made that clear as soon as he arrived at my home in Chicago.

"I will not be here very long," he said. "I have come to die."

Inside of one short week, his statement proved that he had psychic ability, for I was on the train following his body.

But before he left this Earth, he sat in my den, agitatedly puffing a strong cigar. He nearly knocked me out from all the smoke, but he begged me to stay in the room with him for a few moments. I could tell that he was troubled — that he needed to tell me something important.

"Are you going to confess to a murder? Or that you are not my father after all?"

He shook his head. "My name is not Henderson," he said. "It's Minto."

He proceeded to tell me how he started his business career as an office boy in a lithographing establishment at thirteen years of age. Over the course of his life, the only change in his line of work was him becoming the employer instead of the one employed. By the time he turned seventy-six, he bought out every employer and ultimately passed into the Great Beyond as the President. But this is not to say that his career was smooth or easy. He failed in business while we were living in Glasgow, Scotland. In those days, 'failure' meant imprisonment, so my parents gathered all of their children and fled the country. While on the briny deep fearing he might be traced, he assumed the maiden name of his wife, which was Henderson. He never laid claim to his real name after that, and it bothered him dearly.

"I have been living under an alias all of my life," he told me.

From the moment he said the words, I could tell that a

great weight lifted off of him. It seemed he could breathe once more.

"Why do you tell me this?" I asked.

"Lulu, I would like you to see to it that the name on our family lot in Spring Grove is changed from Henderson to Minto."

Of course, I obliged. Not long thereafter, I found my father in his room with his arms outstretched. A wonderful expression of happiness spread over his lately troubled face.

"God," he said, "please take me. I commend my spirit into Your keeping."

I begged him not to talk that way, as I did not want to be parted from my best pal.

"Child, you do not understand. The moment I die will be the most wonderful moment of my life. I will then face my Maker."

Those were the last words my Father ever spoke to me. I did indeed change our family lot from Henderson to Minto, but still I felt that I had to do something to honor my father's true name. I was able to do so the day that a little boy was handed from me, fresh from the oven. No one else had ever fed him, and when only a few hours old, I gave him his first sunbath, in my front yard. As I sat there, my father's dying request came to me. I could hear his words as I looked into the little boy's face.

"And so, Minto," I told the boy, who had stopped sobbing

by now. "I named you in commemoration of my father. And your middle name was my Mother's maiden name. So the next time that someone tells me that you and I are not family, you go ahead and tell them that you carry the family name that I haven't the privilege to bear. How about that?"

Fighting the Welfare Bureau

※❀※

In June of 1932, I received one of those ominous-looking business envelopes with "Welfare Bureau" printed in the upper left corner. Upon perusing the contents, I learned that it was a command for me to be in Los Angeles on a certain date. The complaint against me was that I was allegedly placing children in homes without a license. This piece of paper did not keep me awake. I just thanked God that my record was clean and that I could face "Old Nick" himself with perfect equanimity. Over the next few days, however, I became conscious of a very powerful inner urge to get an attorney.

On the day of the meeting, I found myself at an unusually long director's table, surrounded by females of all sizes, shapes and ages. In this investigation, there were two males: one representing the District Attorney's office, who proudly and significantly tipped back on two hind legs of his chair. This act alone suggested that he was the head of this Vigilance Committee. Now that he was doing it, his word must be law. The other man was supposed to handle me. Each person had the look of satisfaction on their countenance that at last the law had brought the guilty culprit to her knees. In their arms, they held briefcases that they seemed to think contained data relating to undernourished and mistreated humans.

But alas! Things are seldom what they seem, and just so here. Some of the data was so absolutely false that it would seem highly propitious for the one in question to have been on the payroll of a burlesque on "The Nick Harris Detective Agency." There was not one grain of Truth in the charges presented in this meeting.

As I sat there watching these self-satisfied people, I kept looking for the mysterious woman who was "altogether not favorable to me" — the one who had first deemed my work so deplorable. Relayed to me at various times by eminent attorneys, the question she always put to them was when she heard my name was, "Did she ask you for money? Was money mentioned?" The answer was invariably no! But still, she did not believe these claims.

At last she arrived, and the only one for whom I left my seat and heartily smiled when I extended my hand.

"I have always wanted to meet you, but I have been so busy. I have never had time to get over."

She smiled sweetly. What executioner does not when they feel they have the 'goods' on you? While she seated herself, I had a mental picture of the poor souls that I was housing in Pasadena, my little House of Prayer. I thanked God that my work had secured my reputation among the Newspaper men. I recalled the headlines:

"There is a woman in Pasadena who will help."

I could hear the voices of destitute mothers who begged me to look after their babies.

"You can't go back on your promise to me."

"I have nowhere else to turn."

"What would happen to my little one if you abandoned your cause?"

And here I was, facing my accusers.

"Atten-shun!"

A crack of the gavel, and we were off! The one whom I thought was the head of this meeting remained seated. However, the one next to him had a big stack of papers in front of her. She stated her case plainly that I was not licensed to do this work. My attorney then spoke, expressing a desire to know the object of this investigation, and whether what I said might be used against me.

They reassured him that they merely wanted an understanding and to remind me that I could not continue my work as I was doing it. Inwardly, I smiled at the situation because I knew that I had been Divinely Guided. Really and truly, I did not know I had been so busy until I saw that mass of papers on that table. Every page was another case of me saving a life. How ironic that the very charges against me were the concrete evidence of my having benefited humanity! I looked at the stack, disgusted that it had gained such proportion against me. Still, I was confident that there was not one instance that they could possibly scrape up against me.

Nevertheless, they began pelting me with snowballs in the shape of my heart — made up of my love, energy, and unselfish service to humanity. At some point, I had enough and stuck in my own oar. I cannot pretend that I was the one doing the talking — I was merely the instrument, and there is only a little that I remember. I told them that I got my thrill by living the brotherhood of man, and that I had promised God that I would take every baby and child that crossed my path. I told them that their suspicion came from jealousy and their own lack of compassion and love. You should have seen the look that came over my attorney's face!

"My client belongs in the Pulpit, and not in the Nursery," he said to the room.

As these various humanitarian acts piled up against me, I attempted to explain my innocence with logic and reason. But I only received the same response from the chair-tipping man.

"You know the law, and we have to abide by it."

After what felt like an endless loop of useless conversation, the first real charge was presented. The people in the room presented that they suspected that the transfer of money to my name was connected to my work. Could you imagine? After all the love that I showered on my babies; after laying my life down to relay the truth that God lives — I was being accused of being a materialist!

"Who leveraged this accusation?" my attorney asked.

"It is in our notes," the board responded.

He insisted upon holding up the meeting until she found them. The name announced to this assemblage was none other than that of the man who had so persistently suggested "slipping" money into my hand. Why, you might ask? Because he had never heard of a work so wonderful, and he thought that I deserved something for never charging a cent for my services.

"That's very kind of you," I had answered, but I'm all stocked up."

"Please. Let me give you something. The millionaires who have become foster parents of your babies should create a trust fund for you, which would give you an income for the rest of your life."

"Do not stop by my house — I will not be home. Thanks just the same."

All I had in my mind was my responsibility to God. Knowing how God had taught me through visions, my sole objective was to get God's message on the screen where it would make a lasting impression before the largest number of people. I did not care for money — not the slightest bit.

When this worker mentioned that man's name in the

hearing of all of these women, do you suppose I was able to keep from telling the Truth? No — not then, nor now. But the board continued on. They brought up luncheon engagements and asked me if I had purposefully attended for a free meal. If they only knew the reality that my family could not shoo me out of the kitchen long enough for me to sit down for a meal to myself. Here I was to sit like some numbskull and stand for all of this, just because they were licensed welfare workers and I was only a co-worker with God.

"Why do you live this way?" one of them finally said. "If you're so honest, why don't you do as others do and get a license. It does not cost anything. What are you trying to hide?"

I just looked at her. "Why should I waste wind trying to make you understand something that has taken the better part of my life to prove? You could not grasp it, else you would not assume your present attitude."

"Do you mind telling just why you refuse to work under a license?"

"I am writing a book about my work," I answered. "When you buy it, you will get an inkling of what is in my heart and head, and undoubtedly your question will be answered."

See, explaining my reasoning would have had no effect. I never heard of anyone broadcasting an invitation to be your guest, and then on their departure presenting them with a bill. Did you? Imagine having to have a License to express Brotherly love. Obtaining a license would mean that God's license was not enough. That His guidance was not sufficient.

Eventually, the investigation closed. My enemies had thrown everything they had at me, but nothing had stuck to me. As soon as we got out into the hall, my attorney burst out laughing.

"Well girl, you certainly handed them a talk."

"I did not. God did."

"If the Lord had been in that room, He would have agreed with you."

"He was there!" I cried. "That is what no one understands. He has always been with me; I have always been conscious of His presence."

By this time we had reached the auto park and, standing on the corner like a couple of kids who had put something over the school teacher, we gloated over our achievement. Before we parted, the attorney impressed upon me the importance of watching my step.

"If they ever trip you up, they'll soak you with a nice little fine of five hundred dollars."

"A fat chance they have of getting it. If they send me off to jail, at least I'll have the time to finish my book."

I hopped into my car feeling entirely repaid for having braved the lion in his den. I thought of the babies I had at home. Dear little Fritzie Eizenblat. How darling he was at two in the A.M.; how sweetly he always smiled. And little Farina, just too cute for words, which she was beginning to make use of. She would jump up and down until she knocked the bottom out of her bed, and when I'd hear the thump, I'd find her under the springs.

"Bed broke!" she would cry.

I thought back to that dear old doctor in Chicago — the one who knew me better in two hours than my own parents.

"You will not pick a quarrel," he had said. "But you could and would stage a battle royal, if put on the defensive."

The prior hours had proven him correct.

The Hypocrisy of Welfare

PERHAPS MY DISDAIN FOR THE WELFARE DEPARTMENT IS still misunderstood. It comes from hypocrisy, as I have not seen them ever put children first. It is always business and paperwork. Take Minto's bout with tuberculosis, for example. I had want of enrolling him at the Pasadena Preventorium where he could be quarantined until his symptoms ran their course. After being told that he was eligible, I was advised that it would cost me from ten to fifteen dollars per month to house him in the facility.

Now, it had been years since I had any income. I had already sold all the keepsakes that had sentimental value to equip him with shoes, trousers, and bicycle tires! When I told friends of my predicament, I was given a firm piece of advice.

"You are entitled to state aid for those two children, and

you are very foolish not to apply for it. All you have to do is go to City Hall."

I must admit, I had a difficult time letting go of my ideals, as I had long thought of City Hall as my nemesis. But putting my pride in my pocket, I made an appointment with one of thc heads of the Welfare department.

I waited for what seemed an interminable length of time, drying out like a sponge. Every way I turned, there were pictures of our president. The clicking of typewriters told me very plainly that they had not installed Remington Rand's noiseless typing machines. Finally I got an audience.

"This is your first visit up here, isn't it?"

Fully agreeing, and inwardly deciding it would also be my last, I attempted to get information.

"I have been told so many times that these two children are entitled to state aid, and I am ignorant on the subject. So much so that I can never give an intelligent answer, so that is really what I have come for."

The woman looked into her files and approached me again.

"How many babies have you mothered?"

"Over one hundred and sixty over the last twelve years," I replied.

"You must have had over ten in a single year."

"Once, I got eight babies in seven days in a single December. So that week, I celebrated Christmas eight times."

The woman shook her head, bewildered.

"We have renewed your license each year, but we do not have a record of your income. You can't go on living without money. How do you manage, anyway?"

"You do not understand the philosophy that I have put into action. Everything in my life, I have given away. But if I am smart enough to clothe, feed, and put a roof over my children's little heads, what is the necessity of an income?"

"It is clear that your resources are limited."

"That is why I have not legally adopted the children. If I were in a position to support them, I would."

It became quite apparent that my instinct had been correct, and visiting City Hall would not result in any form of relief. And so, I packed my things and headed for the door.

"I will do what I can for you. I will call you this afternoon — I am your friend."

I did not fall for such a statement. To this day I have never received a call, not that I expected to. I headed home and did what I always do. I treated my child on my own, and he recovered. What God wants is red-blooded heart action. Compassionate understanding — not hard-boiled pencil and pad figuring, festooned with endless yards of red tape. Those who pretend to help without lifting a finger are just as useless as the materialists who spend their lives chasing wealth.

Yoric: An Answered Prayer

❧❧❧

ONE SO OFTEN HEARS THE QUESTION: "DO YOU BELIEVE in prayer? Does God answer prayer?"

I want to prove to you how I know God does answer my prayers. The peculiar thing is that I did not need to fall onto my knees in order to pray. You who have been listening to my story must realize by this time that I feel a direct connection with God, through "my babies." At this time, my encounters with welfare workers had dwindled my supply of little ones to two: Gloria and Minto. Of course, I desired to serve more little souls.

"God," I prayed, "I wish you would send me a little child, please, just to show me you still think my work satisfactory. Just a little encouragement, God, because not a living soul understands me."

I hankered for a little, emaciated hungry baby — the kind

that lingers between life and death, sunken eyes, high cheek-bones; the kind that when God lets me touch, I know my life has been right, completely consecrated.

The next day, the telephone rang. It was Margaret, a woman I had helped years earlier.

"The baby isn't well," she exclaimed. "All the neighbors tell me what to do, and each one says something different. I get so upset, and I'm just desperate. I'm nursing him, and he hasn't gained, so I don't think it is doing him any good. He's three months old."

"Come this afternoon, and I will help you."

When Margaret and her poor Yoric arrived, I knew that God had answered my prayer. I know absolutely whereof I speak. That little thing, with his half-closed lids flickering like the dying embers in an old-fashioned log fire; the dried, parched lips dying for some of my food — I knew that I could ease his suffering. There I sat in all my glory, in the corner of the couch with a bottle in my hand and the darling little help-less babe in my arm. As the food flowed in, my thanks poured out.

Giving the Mother some of the food and assuring her that the baby would be alright, I started her off on her way. The next day, I tried to get in touch with her and learned that Yoric was doing splendidly. But then, he contracted a little cold and Margaret brought him back to me. It was some work, adding Yoric to my group of wild little Indians, but I thought I could be the means of saving that little thing's life. And with my understanding, I had no fear. Margaret suggested reimbursing me for the clothes I bought for Yoric, but it was an absolute impossibility for me to accept anything for my service. With my interpretation of my work, it must be my charity, my God-given gift, passed on for the benefit of humanity in the spirit of love.

The baby thrived. He returned to his mother with his dear little cheeks filling out and getting so peppy. Combine the interpretation of my work, faith in God's ability to direct with experience, and what have you? Success.

Nearly Losing My Heart

ONE LATE DECEMBER AFTERNOON, I WAS SITTING IN A barber shop having my little boy's hair cut. Gloria was beside me, taking it all in and amusing herself with a big stuffed dog.

A woman entered with her young 'hopeful,' and in keeping with all proud mothers, we began comparisons. One remark led to another until it was clear that this woman's child had once been one of my own! I gave a look of satisfaction, as one of my 'flock' emerged from the chair, all spick and span, with his big, round and roguish blue eyes. With a broad grin, he bounded up onto my lap.

"I love my Sweekark mother." Then in the dearest little confidential query, "Do you like how I look?"

His beaming smile had always been a bright spot when he knew he had put one over on me, and the cute way he said 'Goriu,' with his well-formed mouth. And then I recalled how

I had found their little blonde heads together, when the unusual silence made me wonder what they were up to.

'Goriu' was now loudly whispering into her newly found brother's ear, as kindly as ever. With a gamut of emotion and recollection running riot, the woman in the barber shop asked the inevitable question.

"Is he for adoption?"

How I dreaded the sound of it. But every little boy is entitled to and should have a father. It seemed it would have been so much easier for me had he not been with me so long, but it was the length of time that I had 'mothered' him that had changed him into this exceptional child. In a very few days his expression had changed completely from a surly looking tough youngster in thread bare overalls, that craved love, but which I soon discovered had been a minus quantity. He turned into the most voluptuous manchild that has ever come to my door. As we sat there waiting for the other haircut, I made the desperate break;

"I might possibly part with him if the right home turned up, but I'd like nothing better than to keep him myself. I realize he should have a father, though, and to be settled permanently."

The woman nodded in understanding. As we separated, I gave a clear, final remark.

"If you happen to have a real friend who wants a regular little man, let me know."

That evening, as I was giving my three little children their repast, the phone rang. I was surprised to hear the voice of the woman I had met that afternoon. She wanted to come down at once; she insisted on having her husband see 'that darling little boy.' They might adopt him themselves!

This was too sudden; I wouldn't disturb the children, as it was past their bedtime. I agreed, however, to call her later in the week. Each little thing that he did seemed sweeter, and I went to bed that night with a decided heartache. I had no one in this material world to cheer me or to give me courage. It was all a part of the service that no one understood, not having the slightest inkling of the undercurrent in my work.

The couple visited and ultimately decided that they would rather have a little girl. So then, in a way I was happy again. But still, something ate at me. Standing in the threshold of my kitchen door, where most of my spiritual experiences took place, I turned to God.

"God, here are my three little children to do with as you see fit. I can no longer stand the strain of knowing whether to keep or send them away to another help. I need Your help; I am resigned."

After I had put the children to bed and turned out the lights, the phone rang. The voice was one I had not heard for a very long time, and I wondered why he should be calling me. We had nothing in common, so after discussing everything under the sun, the man blurted out his true reason for calling.

"I want Gloria!"

If that request had been shot out of a canon, with a five minute interval between each word, it could not have struck me more forcibly. It would be impossible for me to give you a correct interpretation of my feelings, or to number the various angles that it presented to my mind.

But in spite of how much I wanted to tell the man off, my case presented itself to me fully. Less than two hours before, I had asked God to help me. Had I a right to dictate to God how that help was to come to me? In a flash, I was reminded that I was being tested.

"Well, alright. You can come over tomorrow afternoon at three o'clock. I'll let you see her."

The morning was arranged. I had no idea what would come of it — my all consuming effort and thought was based on how and where I would stand before The Great Tribunal! And while it may sound insane to you who are listening to this story, many a time I have been reminded that Jesus was getting a laugh, or giving me a smile at the various situations that arose between the servant and man. The man arrived with two women to help guide the interaction.

As the party emerged from their high-powered limousine and came into my play yard, I happened to be standing in the doorway. The peculiar part is I could always see from the other person's viewpoint. I could understand how my play yard, all upside down and dried up to keep childrens' feet dry, would make these people turn inside out. They were used to green, velvety lawns and every tiny thing in order. They did not know that this unpretentious looking building was my House of Prayer. They did not know how hard I had tried to keep these three last children, nor how, in desperation, I had placed them at the feet of God.

They came into the living room where they found the children. I looked one woman over, attempting to discover something that was "queer," but failed. I watched in agony as they spoke with my little Gloria. If she had gone willingly, I would have thought it was intended. I had nothing to do with her answer; I left that in God's Hands. I did think that if it were intended for me to part with Gloria, the man should take Minto, also. Let me have one last heart-ache; I could not stand two more tugs at my heart. But the man only had room for one little girl.

"Why don't you keep on with your work?" she asked me. "It must be agony to have children continually pulled from your heart."

No one but God could understand. I felt ready to drop on the floor, curl up, and never awaken.

"I have gone my limit," I said. "I have arrived at the end of the lane, and I am so tired I could not wash and iron for another child, no matter how much I might want to!"

"Do you do all their laundry?"

"Well, who do you suppose does it? I've spent so much money I couldn't afford to have it done."

They inveigled me into letting them take two of my three children, presumably to spend the Christmas holidays. What mother does not like to have her children have a good time? So, as I have never wanted to stand in anyone's light, I let them go. No thought was taken of my Christmas, for which I was all prepared, having bought their toys. The moment they left the house, all desire to trim a tree was completely killed. The next day, I phoned the various places where I had bought some rather expensive toys, and they very considerately took them back.

In the end, my heartaches and principles got the best of me. I insisted on the return of my little girl, to the complete consternation of the wealthy man. And so, I smashed the tentative plans of a man who could not understand why his will should be upset. I brought my little child home, where she belonged. That is one move that I would never have made had I worshipped the so-called Almighty Dollar.

Weeks after this had all blown over, one of the women who had met with Gloria phoned me.

"You should not do all that house work; take care of the children, try to write a book, and have all the financial strain. When I meet deserving people, I try to help them, I have my own children, so I do not want any of yours, but this is wonderful work. I'd be glad to help toward the support of Gloria and Minto."

To think that it would be a woman — not a man — who would lift me up in my darkest hour! Now, we all have our individual definitions of a friend. To some, it is the one who turns up at the opportune time with a drink! To another, food; others, amusement. Mine, however, was something so entirely different, so unheard of. It was a person who was just as queer as I was. Someone who put aside material loss in order to serve God. To that one friend, I send my heartfelt and sincere thankfulness. I will always know her as the Angelic Messenger of Holmby Hills.

Politics & God

IT HAS TAKEN ME TWELVE YEARS OF EARNEST, PATIENT, unselfish devotion to learn that when one is loyal to God, it is an absolute impossibility to be disloyal to one's country. For when man recognizes and consequently experiences that intimate relationship of God as his Father, it becomes clear that all other humans are his brothers and sisters. And this knowledge prevents man from harming his brothers and sisters, for they are part of his family. God never directed man to slaughter that babe made in His own image.

Before there is any great stride toward World Peace, the people will have to discard some of their man-made laws that permit vice and corruption. They will have to acknowledge God and His wondrous Power as the Alpha and Omega, paying their debt to Him by trampling the so-called almighty dollar. Currency has its uses, but it should always take a secondary place when striving for a higher purpose. As soon as every man and woman has peace in his or her heart, God will make the rest possible. When more people aspire to live a Christlike existence, there will be less time for conjecture as to interpretation of His teachings and His so-called miracles. Until we purge ourselves of all selfishness, we will not be able to understand. But when we do, we will all agree that it is worth the effort.

All one has to do is to look back to the World War. Such enthusiasm! Such patriotism! Such unison of thought and action! Each for his own side. It meant death to one, if victory were accorded the other. And we all saw what power man was given to wield for what was right. Death came in such appalling numbers. The hearts of mothers and fathers were irreparably crushed. If humanity's heart aches, even in the knowledge of victory, we must eradicate the repetition of such wholesale slaughter of God's children. War is nothing more nor less than legalized murder.

If man wishes to atone the wrongs he has done; if man wishes to replace heartache with happiness — let him condemn any act that would make him ashamed to face his Maker. Let him face God with love in his heart, with the desire to do that which is best in him. For under the guidance of God, man would surely not kill his neighbor to gain earthly so-called riches, which is a misnomer in reality.

Instead of waiting for so-called patriotism to rescue us, we must try joining together when a war is not raging. Then, see what strides will be made towards world peace. I know whereof I speak. Do you suppose that an ordinary woman would have been able to carry on successfully, through these years of intensive work, if love and service had not been her sole objective? God made everything I attempted possible because the right motive was in my heart. Just so with world peace.

As a nation, we are living and acting a lie. Everyone in this world knows our faith is placed in the so-called almighty dollar. And instead of caring for others, we only care for ourselves. There is nothing man likes better than to look at himself. That must change to looking *within* himself. If man could be earnest and sincere, he would instantaneously connect with God. As an experiment, if everyone in this world padlocked their machines and devices, focusing their attention upon God, they would recognize the latent energy lying dormant in their bodies. When God sees we are sufficiently honest to make these adjustments, see how quickly He would come to the rescue. Our world could be transformed if we worked under the immutable Law of God with nothing but the much advertised but little used "Love Thy Neighbor as Thyself" stamped indelibly in each individual heart. And none of us would ever want to return to the old system that we occupy today. If you crave World Peace, you will all have to buckle down. After all, World Peace is Individual Peace, multiplied by as many people as there are in the world. The idea is as simple as rolling off a log.

Do you suppose if this were a spiritual age, that my life with "my babies" would have been anything to be classed as out of the ordinary? Why, no. Everyone would be trying to do something for someone else. It would be such a common occurrence to see a woman who loved babies.

I wouldn't exchange for the grandest, most stately church service and everything that goes with it — topped off with the most learned minister's recognition of me — for just any of the experiences that I have had with my babies. From the experiences I have had and the satisfaction in my heart, I know absolutely that God simply wants devotion and service. The fact that I have successfully reared so many babies, and was just as much enthusiastic at the end of the twelfth year as I was when I started, should excite the curiosity of independent thinkers across the world.

If I can get as many interested in God as are in Pee-wee Golf, Jigsaw Puzzles minded, or the Funnies, then my life will have been worth it. If the entire world would use one-tenth the time in attempting to tune in with God as they do in trying to hear a prizefight, we would find how instantaneously God answers the call. If we got as much upset when we knew that something had gone wrong with our Spiritual Radios as we did when the battery has run down, the world would be a much more peaceful place. The reason that there is so much unhappiness, so much unrest, is because people are following material pleasures, and all things material come to an end.

Prove by your actions rather than by word of mouth. Each human being has some way of expressing their appreciation of all of God's wonderful gifts. It is not how much one does, but the spirit in which one does it. Aspire to spiritual understanding. See for yourself, Truth as it has been taught this servant. Anyone can be just as supremely happy as I have been by applying the same set of rules. Have faith in God, offer your services, and be content in the knowledge that He is able to direct you. Do not wish for anything that he does not wish for you to have. Place your trust in Him and be happy in that fact alone. God will take care of the rest.

An Illuminating Encounter with a Phrenologist

WHEN AN AVALANCHE OF THOUGHTS BEGAN TO CHASE through my mind, I likened my head unto that of a big house with a lot of rooms. These rooms were my brain and my cells. Of course, some people get along with much less space. Some even manage an entire life using the garage, never realizing that within them lies dormant that wonderful Power to open up as big an establishment as one may choose. It's up to the individual how large of a house he would like to live in.

Being well developed along those lines, I began to figure that I would see a phrenologist to ascertain if there were any new developments when it came to my mind. Now, I had long been skeptical of doctors, and I had good reason. The lot of them had told me terrible things over the years. Once upon a time, a very high-brow M.D. told me very emphatically that when I reached the so-called climacteric — usually a pivotal point for worry in every woman's mind past middle age — that I would lose my mental faculties and the very first to desert me would be my memory. I am not going to tell you what I thought of such an inhuman remark, which was made to put fear in me and thus keep me a patient for life, but this is what I answered, whilst snickering.

"I am going to begin to lose my memory right now by forgetting that God ever made anything quite so foolish as a man who would thus attempt to intimidate me."

He colored quite perceptibly, then laughingly attempted to offset it. But in this episode of my life, I decided to give doctors another try. I thought that if tendencies are registered to sufficiently change the contour of one's head, then there would certainly be some noticeable differences in mine after twelve years of struggle and self-sacrifice. So in my peculiar way of getting a thrill on this earth-plane, I went.

"Do people change, so that it is noticeable in the measurements of their head?" I asked the doctor.

"Certainly. The entire blood supply is renewed in from two to four weeks. If it weren't, one would die."

"Do you remember that I was here at least ten years ago?"

"Yes. You're the woman who always had to be working, always busy doing for someone else."

"That's right, and I'm still at it; I have reared, mothered, and handled in the neighborhood of one hundred and sixty-eight babies, all alone, and now I'm trying to write a book about my work.

"That should be interesting."

"Yes, but the funny thing is that there's a lot about God in my book. Do you believe in God?"

"Yes, I do. Maybe not the same interpretation that you have, but we know there is a Supreme being."

"Do you know anything about the Inner Voice? Do you know God talks to people?"

"No. I don't know anything about that."

"Well then, you can't do me any good; I'm trying to find someone who can understand me.

"I am not developed along those lines. But just because I'm color blind, I don't say there is no such thing as color. I don't happen to have it, while you have that vast development in the spiritual region and in the area of ideality. I told you ten years ago that you had enough love to spread all over the world, and even that's increased. Your line of thought has certainly been forcing blood up into these other cells, which now show development."

All this time he was taking measurements. When he mentioned "that vast spiritual area," I immediately thought of a ballpark and my first child being a "Babe Ruth." I figured all the "home runs" I'd been making. So you see, I was interested in studying my own mind, and I was sufficiently foolish to feel I was arriving at something.

"How is it possible that I have seen things that other people cannot see?" I asked.

"You must be psychic. That is some of your Spiritual development asserting itself."

No wonder I liked the phrenologist. Before leaving, I asked this especially gifted doctor, a final question. A rather simple question, but difficult to answer.

"Now, what do you advise me to do?"

"You are absolutely impossible to change now. That is something that you will have to handle yourself."

Spending two very interesting hours with this Doctor, and though he discovered different developments, he was still sorry that I did not read or study.

"You are arriving at the age where you can not continue this activity. And with the wonderful brain you have, you could absorb in a short time what would take others a lifetime to figure out."

Well, my mind went to the types of books that line shelves. All books, of course, are not made equal. If books are the means of producing thoughts, and thoughts are the means of providing sustenance for brain cells, it is troubling how often grisly crimes and murders are emphasized in literature, or even news. It is sufficiently harmful to publish detailed accounts of things so blood curdling and repulsive. In place of murder mysteries, why not fill the daily papers with the so-called mysteries or miracles performed by Christ while He was on earth? Why not open up what should prove to be the Main Highway — a wonderful boulevard system leading straight to God? Try nourishing uninhabited brain cells by ferreting the spiritual interpretation of the Bible.

I left the Doctor, still regretting that I had not seen things as he had attempted to guide me twelve years before. But I figured that through concentrated application, I had discovered that which many had been doubtful about for nearly two thousand years — the Reality of God. To the "pooh-poohers" of phrenology, I have this to say in its defense. The doctor who used only a tape measure on my cranium came so close to discovering the real me. He understood that I wanted to be a bridge for the benefit of humanity. It is true — I always wanted to be that — but materialists attempted to remodel me into a moving stairway. He also told me I would deal with people who would naturally overestimate their own importance, and that I would have to draw heavily on my ability to overlook their smallness.

"With your great amount of love," he advised, "it will be easy for you to pity their lack of your wonderful gift."

That man certainly knew his business and proved to be a modern prophet.

The Seance

You'd be surprised to know how happy and interesting one's life can be with a mind as supposedly "dotty" as mine. I thank God for this special brew of insanity. It has helped me in every difficulty and placed me in a position where I could laugh aloud at the "sane" materialist who overlooks the main point of contact: God. I know that all of my spiritual experiences help me to understand what the world is all about, as the same things happen today as they did when Jesus trod this plane. It is just that people are so busy chasing will o' the wisps that they cannot get their Spiritual apparatus in working order. The average person would rather sit through three hours of "The Cat and The Canary" than to concentrate on the "little Birdie" in their own wonderful soul.

Over the course of my life, I have always tried to act upon impulses that may seem irrational to others, but are God-directed in my opinion. For example, while walking past a railway station with my daughter and her baby in Glencoe, Illinois, I suddenly got the feeling that I needed to visit my aunt in Fort Wayne. Where this feeling came from, I cannot say. But I felt it, and so I decided to embrace it.

The aunt in question was my father's favorite sister. It occurred to me that though he had been gone from this plane for ten years, he may have directed me to see her. At that very moment, as plain and distinct as if my father were there with me, I felt him kiss me on the lips. I was not the only one who felt his presence. When I arrived at the station and my aunt picked me up, she made her thoughts known.

"You know," she started, "I have the strongest feeling that your Father is here with us."

Now, this is a queer experience that a rationalist would perhaps cast aside. But how could they be sure that my father was not at the wheel in this episode? Instead of constantly saying no, I just kept a-going, open to the thrill of the next reel.

The next morning, my aunt naturally asked me about the shape of my story.

"You'll have to judge for yourself," I answered. "I have had so many important experiences, and I don't know how to explain them. Like when Papa visited when Kenzie passed on."

"I remember that time," my aunt said. "When he returned from Chicago to Cincinnati, he told me that you had told him something that he did not understand. You said that you had felt something that you could not articulate, and that perhaps you could recount it in a few weeks' time."

That, of course, was the feeling that I needed to carry out my baby work. My father had been there with me when I felt the spark of God in July 1915. That day, which had no markings of anything out of the ordinary, ended up being remarkably special. For as we were thinking of something to do, my cousin came up with an idea that would provide a transcending experience.

"There's a woman in town who gets messages," she said. "Why don't I telephone her and see if she can come here?"

At the time, I hadn't the faintest clue what she meant by "messages." Nonetheless, we obliged the idea and accepted the woman's invitation to join her circle. I must say, I did not immediately take the afternoon seriously as I didn't understand what was liable to happen.

The medium was a little, emaciated looking thing. She did not charge anything for her services — just a jar for optional donations, should we feel compelled to reach into our purses.

"Will we all receive messages?" I asked.

"I can't say. We must wait until the seance is over."

I had never heard of a seance! Born in 1875, and now 1929! God was certainly taking His own time in opening my eyes to the world.

She put on a record with all sorts of noises — singing,

chanting, a blaring trumpet. There were twelve of us one who sat in this darkened room. The medium explained that if a spirit greeted us, we should return the greeting just as if we had met on the street. We were to treat these spirit friends exactly like human beings, as that would raise the vibrations that made it possible for them to communicate with us. Not a bit of this excited me. I sat there unconcerned, mentally criticizing the terrible mixture of voices. I wondered how anything could happen with such discord.

After the singing had gone on for a while, the ladies on the other side of the circle began to chat with their loved ones. They asked all kinds of questions and received satisfactory answers in many different types of voices. One lady sang a song in German with her husband. His was distinctly a man's voice, and the words were very plain. She explained it was his favorite song, and she seemed to be intensely happy to be in communion with him. Just as they had in Earth life, he sang alto and she soprano.

Every now and then, a little spirit girl would bob up with a laughing voice. It was her work, I deduced, to keep the other spirits peppered up. If they began to lag, or if it became hard for us to hear them, she would strengthen them and their voices would grow stronger.

Such merriment and intense happiness came from the other side of the circle. I, being a complete stranger to the seance, was perfectly content to just listen. Not for one second did I expect to be in any way recognized.

Suddenly, a very heavy, masculine voice announced his presence among us. He greeted us as a body and said he would return later to answer questions.

"That's Doctor Deaton," the medium explained. "He was selfish in his Earth life, neglecting to give help to suffering humanity when he could, so he tries to make amends."

The circle proceeded to sing songs in all keys. They were all of a religious nature, and when I realized that one more tuneless voice certainly couldn't make a very great difference, I joined. Suddenly, I felt enthused in my discordant notes.

"There are three strange ladies in our circle this afternoon," the little spirit girl said. "The pretty little lady with the white hair has been all around over here."

I did not wish to be conceited, as there were other white-haired ladies in the circle. But then, the people around me clarified that I was the one being targeted by the spirit.

"You live a long way from here," the spirit said.

"Yes. I live in California."

"You love little children, don't you?"

"I do."

"You have a little boy over here in the spirit world."

"How old was he when he left this world?"

"He was half past seventeen. He would like to sing for you."

And so, to my disbelief, my Kenzie sang three verses of "Precious Jewels." He had never been able to carry a tune. It had always been one of our laughs. As I sat there, with my right arm resting on the chair and my hand up to my face, I regarded my son.

"Kenzie?"

"Yes, mother. Take your hand down from your face and let me shake hands with you."

The room was so pitch-dark that it was impossible for me to see anything. I couldn't even see my own hand right in front of me. Only spiritual sight could penetrate that darkness.

"Mother, you hold me too close to you. You hold me too tight. Do you realize that I have never been away from you?"

"Yes, Kenzie, I've always felt you were with me. Say, do you know what I am doing? Can you see me?"

"Yes, Mother. Stick to your book until it is finished."

"Kenzie, I'll stick to it if it takes me another twelve years. I promise you that."

He then gave a contented little chuckle, which I recognized so well.

"Aunt Jessie, you do not look any older than when last met."

Jessie got it into her head that she would quiz him to see if his memory was equally retentive.

"Do you remember when you visited us in Hartwell?"

"Yes, I remember that I was happy all day. But when night came, I was homesick for my mother, and I cried."

"Yes, Kenzie. You did cry for her. Do you remember me asking you what you called canned goods?"

"Yes, Aunt Jessie. Tinned goods, not canned. Aunt Jessie, do you remember when I nearly choked to death? I ran out in the yard with a fistfull of stolen cookies. I tried to swallow them before you could see me, which brought on a coughing fit."

How we all laughed at that. And then, before leaving us again, my son addressed me for a final time.

"Mother, there are all kinds of love. That of father and mother, brother and sister, lover and sweetheart, but no love like my mother has for me. Mother and child."

Thus is my account for the wonderful demonstration I had with my child. In my heart was the most sincere thankfulness to God for giving me this positive proof that there is no death. Some may think that this experience was the result of hallucination, but I will not be fooled out of my own child's voice. God had directed me onto that train to Fort Wayne and into that circle.

After the experience in Fort Wayne, I thought I would see what would happen in California, just for the fun of it. And so, I went to an absolutely unknown place among complete strangers, where a minister of the gospel was holding his own seance. Not long after the seance began, I was plucked out of the circle.

"There is a doctor who wants to say something to you."

Now, after leaving the medium's circle in Fort Wayne, my aunt, cousin, and I had all agreed that if we ever heard the voice of Doctor Deaton again, we would recognize it. It was that powerful and outstanding.

"What is his name?" I asked.

"He says he is Dr. Deat — Dean — I just can't get hold of it."

As suddenly and unexpectedly as a bomb might explode and without further ado, the same voice carried across the room.

"Why, hello there Mrs. Sullivan, don't you remember me? Dr. Deaton, from way back east? Glad to talk to you again."

The doctor was not the only familiar voice that I would hear that afternoon. Soon, a woman purporting to be a mother joined the room.

"Lucy, I am sorry I talked to you the way I did, when you were a little girl. I did not understand you. Papa and I see you in your little home with all of your babies and all of your work and so many beautiful flowers on your dining room table."

One can imagine what this meant to me, given the trauma of my youth. And so, that afternoon brought peace to my relationship with my mother.

I cannot pretend to know how these seances work. I can only say that they worked for me. And at the end of my baby work, I am blessed that God exposed me to the miracle of communing with those who have left our earthly plane, as doing so brought me much peace.

Understanding Kenzie's Passing

❧❀❧

My real heartache has come in associating Kenzie's passing from earth life with my earnest appeal for God to give me all the babies I want. This has caused the terror that still remains my secret. Was Kenzie taken as a sacrifice, or was it already a matter of record? Was this opportunity to mother my babies, which eventually proved to be a direct medium to God, simply the means for my own salvation? Was it just a practical religion?

No one will ever know how I have longed to talk to someone who could explain it all to me. I wanted to tell some minister what my spiritual experiences have been so as to relieve my troubled heart. On the other hand, I did not want the result of some educated persons' ideas to confuse me. On the night of April 30th, 1928, before the sandman overtook me, I begged for enlightenment.

"God, why can't I look back to July 27th without terror in my heart? What is it that makes me stumble?"

Instantaneously, there flashed a little Sunday School card before me. Upon it, it read, "Ask and ye shall receive; seek and ye shall find; knock and it shall be opened unto you".

Being tired, I fell asleep with those thoughts in my mind. But upon awakening, my first realization of consciousness! I envisioned a winding road, which started at the Day Nursery that Kenzie and I had visited that June day in 1915. The place where we picked up the first child I looked after — David — and brought him to our home on Kenesaw Terrace. Both the Nursery and our house stood out in bold relief. That entire trip was more plainly impressed upon me than a human hand could have made possible, for in that picture it was revealed that I had overlooked the beginning of my work. I lay there stunned for a few moments. Nothing like this had ever happened to me, but it surely was my answer to the question I had asked the night before because my feeling of thankfulness followed immediately.

Our wonderful, All-knowing and All-loving Heavenly Father answered not the question put by word of mouth, but that which had been gnawing at my heartstrings all these years.

"I did not take your child because you had offered him to me," He told me. "I took that opportunity to test your love. When you went for the child in the nursery and through its laughter you were to have your happiness, I put in its place a little, sick, ordinary child. If in your heart you had mother-love — attributes of which are unselfishness and service — you would be attracted to him. But if you decided a sickly child was too much trouble and went home empty-handed, you would prove that your love for Me was not sincere. When the sad day came, and then the very last moment of your child's life on Earth, you further proved your mother-love. If, when your child was taken, you rebelled, thinking it was not fair to take a well boy with a promising future and everything to live for, you would have proven unable to do the necessary work. But in keeping your sorrow to yourself and tripling your energy towards the children in need, you proved your earnestness to serve me. I rewarded you by transforming your little children."

The understanding of these words relieved me of the feeling that I was responsible for Kenzie's death. It ceased to be an added heartache. For the first time, I saw the connection. I felt for the first time in thirteen years an intense happiness that I could not explain. It was a wonderful, unexpected gift from God.

When I came from the nursery that day with that sick boy in my arms, something had taken possession of me. Ever since, I have felt as though I were being carried by "unseen hands," a lightness of heart, and an earnest desire to serve God. Ever since, I have been working, walking, and talking with Him.

A few days after this revelation, on the afternoon of May

5th, 1928, I happened to be one of an assemblage that had gathered in a spirit of love to prove interest in the opening of a private hospital. We were all, to a more or less degree, in an exhilarated condition, due to the flow of general good spirit (not in bottles, however). I especially was interested in this undertaking. One of the doctors had been instrumental in saving the life of one of my children and was always ready to serve me at a moments' notice. This afternoon was my opportunity to show her a little appreciation for the many things she had done for me, so I had all the pretty baskets that had been sent to me on various occasions filled with California's choicest flowers. I paid special attention to one large basket, filling it with lavender and pastel shades until it was beautiful. This card read as follows:

"In memory of McKenzie Lowndes: July 1915 — May, 1928"

There was one tiny basket that looked only big enough to place on a desk, and it looked insignificant when these other baskets were filled. But then, my eye caught upon a calendar and I realized the date. It was one day after the eighth anniversary of my father's passing from this earth. I looked again at the little basket and could not bear to cast it off.

"I cannot help what they think of me. My dead are not dead, and I want them with me this afternoon and I cannot forget nor overlook my father and my mother."

So I called the florist to fill it with Forget-Me-Nots, and

wrote a card that read: "In memory of my Father and Mother." Then, I felt radiantly happy — as if I was walking on air — and drove down to the hospital to deliver the baskets. It all meant so much to me. Standing in the midst of a bevy of buzzing women, those mute baskets told me that the spirit of my father, mother, and child were with me. Life is never dreary, dull, or drab when God furnishes the individual with rose-colored glasses.

I retired earlier than usual that evening. The day had been hot, and I felt the nerve strain due to clutchings at my heart. While at the florist's that morning, I had been hardly able to hold the pen while writing the cards. At home, I felt so dizzy that I had to hold myself when going through the hall, as if I were a balloon breaking away from its moorings. I felt so electrified, much as though I were a human battery, and every spark emanating from me meant power, if properly harnessed. I was reaching out for something, and felt intoxicated — my own strength consuming me. Being tired out, I fell sound asleep.

At three AM on May 6th, 1928, I awakened quite placidly, although my heart had been pounding and racing like mad. It was sufficient to call for help, but I recognized that this intensified acceleration was due to the ether, like the high altitude of a mountain, to which my soul had flown and taken refuge. I was not in the least frightened. Rather, I was awed at a funnel-shaped cloud and its intense brightness all around me. The California sunshine paled in comparison to this light. I seemed to be engulfed in it, and instinctively I knew that I was aware of the light's penetrating and soothing qualities not through my sense of sight, but through my sense of feeling. This I did not think strange. I knew that I was in the Spiritual Presence of God.

"God," I pleaded, "don't make me go back. I know that it was You who gave me my message. Yes, God, I will tell the people that you live; that there is no death. I want to mind You, but please don't make me go back."

Quietly and calmly, I saw the receding end of that funnel-shaped cloud, farther and farther in the distance, with everything distinctly impressed on my mind. My heart felt perfectly normal, but I had the most sickening sensation that I was again on this mundane sphere. I had just glimpsed the land of the living (so-called Dead) where my message was further impressed upon me, and I was being forced against my inner feeling back into this world to deliver it. My heartache was caused by the realization that I was so much happier there than here. For days, I did not recover from this feeling of depression, though I was thankful that I had never disturbed Kenzie's sojourn by hysterical tears in that wonderful ether where we must go eventually. And always, I kept the subconscious thought: "I knew there is no death." It was this substantiation of my intuitive knowledge that carried me on the crest of the wave, no matter what I faced.

By being privileged to feel I was in the Spiritual Presence of God and allowed that glimpse into Eternity, I accepted the wonderful reward for my labor of love. See, God was giving me the assurance that my work had been right. How else could God reward me for a life voluntarily laid down? I could not be paid in money at the end of such a wonderful existence. My craving for Spiritual development had been proven, and I had the feeling that I had reached a very satisfactory conclusion. Honestly and steadfastly living as I have attempted, one is definitely conscious of wonderful rays of love that take possession of the explorer. This clothes him with different knowledge than one ordinarily finds: the knowledge that will make everything possible, eventually. I am pushing on toward that knowledge.

How many remember their first school days when they learned to count on little colored balls strung on wires across the top of the desks? After we finished with them, they were not destroyed, but preserved for others to teach them how to count. So, when God read my heart and knew I had always idealized babies, He supplied me with babies. Attempting to satiate the craving in my heart, He rewarded me with definite knowledge of His ways and developed my mother's love. So, in a way, I have partly discovered why babies were sent to me.

I was tested many times, often doing the things He told me to do, or showed me to do, without knowing why. No human being ever had that power over me. If God had not manifested unto me, this life would have never occurred as it did. One of the most important qualities was my ability to listen. Had I been as unimpressionable as the concrete, I could not have lived this life. It took the hourly training of fifteen years to make my gifts possible.

Now, if each foster parent will give twelve years of unselfish service, she will also learn God's so-called mysterious ways. The glorious satisfaction that fills one working in the interest of one's fellowman, for God, will tell to each human heart a story that cannot be put in words. Perhaps that is why so many of my babies have been directed to homes of wealth.

A Life Well-Lived

❧❦❧

IF I WERE A SHIP, THE PASSING SAILOR WOULD BE ABLE TO tell that I've spanned many nautical miles. He would also be able to tell that I could span many more with some repairs.

"Touch up her flying jib with a bit of carmen," he might say. "Keep her topsail white, as it is her flag of truce that enables her to get in touch with peace advocators, and yet keep at arms' length, pirates, and marauders. She prefers 'to look her age' because she realizes it is impossible to act it."

Now when the ship was finally junked, it would be her secret wish to be returned to her Maker's house where her parts had been assembled and her attributes were thoroughly understood.

There came a time when God miraculously injected prescience into my Being. He showed me that my baby work was at an end, and in its place, He gave me His Message. If I had not been God-directed and God-protected, how else would I have continued my work from 1915 to 1927? How else would I have handled and mothered 168 babies and children over twelve years? Not until 1932 was I corralled. I had been fed as much spiritual food as I could comfortably digest, and I was so thoroughly content with my findings, I was willing to submit to a halt. When my mission was fulfilled and I was ready to progress, it was God who stopped my baby work — Not man.

It is plain to be seen why someone like me, outside of the pulpit, would be chosen to live this life. I had no ulterior motive or desire for personal aggrandizement, and the more I was left alone, the better I liked it. That state of affairs would be highly deleterious to any minister dependent upon his congregation, with popularity and personality being the key note to any well-organized and commercially thriving church. But my church was not built upon the false bottom of glittering gold, but upon my sincere love of God.

In my visions of God, I have experienced the proof of the thing hoped for. That is the reward for the living of this life. If only I were an artist and could transfer my impression of His wonderful smile, His soul-searching eyes, his magnetic and dynamic personality, then would I be able to fulfill in its entirety, the objective of this life. This book will have to suffice.

My dream has always been to live in a little dream nursery where love ruled. God has turned that dream into a reality. Through my practical life with my babies, God in His power has taught me the things that I craved to know. He is all-wise. When He has a Message to deliver to His people, He avoids the pitfalls of misunderstanding and ensures that his disciple is never alone. This servant had but one life to lay down, and she did so willingly. She did not go through this life with the hangdog air of a martyr, but rather in a state of supreme happiness, radiance, and rapturous joy. She has learned that heaven is not a place, but a condition of the mind.

With no cooperation from man, I have had a terrible uphill struggle. This provides all the more reason for non-believers to know that only God has made it possible for me to keep going. Only the realization of the little lives I was saving and the happiness I was spreading has made it worth-while. My readers should not be taken aback or intimidated by such adversity. I assure you, God did not give me anything that I could not handle. I always had the privilege of having a burden that I could bear.

As the composite result of other spiritual experiences, I have been made to understand that my baby days are over. And so I have poured everything into this book. I know that things do not happen haphazardly in God's realm. He has a time for everything. Twenty years has passed since this journey started, and seven years since I was divinely commanded to tell the people that I LIVE. And so, I do not have the slightest inclination to hurry through my work. For

God does not sponsor things of mushroom growth. His examples must stand the test of time. It has taken all of this time to make the child understand, but no longer than God intended it should.

Still, I look back on that day in 1915 when I sat beside the bath and first heard the voice of God.

"Do this. You do this for Me."

And I am proud that I have followed that order. When the World is filled with an intense earnest desire to serve Him and cooperate with Him, then will people reap the blessings of joy, happiness and peace which are their rightful heritage.

Made in the USA
Monee, IL
20 April 2022

95098447R00184